ZEALOUS

7 COMMITMENTS FOR
THE DISCIPLESHIP OF
THE NEXT GENERATIONS

DAVID MICHAEL

PRODUCTION:
Managing Editor: Steve Watters
Designers: Daniel Carroll (cover)
and Laura Johns (interior)
Editorial Review: Karen Hieb, Sally Michael,
Sherri Moran, Jill Nelson, and Candice Watters
Theological Review: Gary Steward

*Zealous: 7 Commitments for the Discipleship
of the Next Generations*

First printing 2020; Second printing 2021.
Published in the United States of America by Truth78.

ISBN: 978-1-7330097-8-2

*Equipping the Next Generations to
Know, Honor, and Treasure God*

Truth78.org
info@Truth78.org
877.400.1414
@Truth78org

To all who are faithfully laboring for the discipleship of the next generation.

Give ear, O my people, to my teaching;
    incline your ears to the words of my mouth!
I will open my mouth in a parable;
    I will utter dark sayings from of old,
things that we have heard and known,
    that our fathers have told us.
We will not hide them from their children,
    but tell to the coming generation
the glorious deeds of the LORD, and his might,
    and the wonders that he has done.

He established a testimony in Jacob
    and appointed a law in Israel,
which he commanded our fathers
    to teach to their children,
that the next generation might know them,
    the children yet unborn,
and arise and tell them to their children,
    so that they should set their hope in God
and not forget the works of God,
    but keep his commandments;
and that they should not be like their fathers,
    a stubborn and rebellious generation,
a generation whose heart was not steadfast,
    whose spirit was not faithful to God.

PSALM 78:1-8

Contents

Part I: What is Zeal and Why Does it Matter?   9

Part II: The 7 Commitments for the   21
Discipleship of the Next Generations

1 ▾ Embrace a Biblical Vision for   23
the Faith of the Next Generation

2 ▾ Foster a Robust Partnership   35
Between Church and Home

3 ▾ Teach the Breadth and Depth   45
of the Whole Counsel of God

4 ▾ Proclaim the Glorious   53
Gospel of Jesus Christ

5 ▾ Disciple the Mind,   61
Heart, and Will

6 ▾ Pray with Dependence   73
on God's Sovereign Grace

7 ▾ Inspire Worship of God,   83
for the Glory of God

Part III: Do Not Lose Heart   93

Acknowledgements 101

Appendix 1 105
Resources Supporting Commitments

Appendix 2 109
Vision for the Next Generations
(Sample Vision Statement)

Appendix 3 119
10 Essential Gospel Truths

Appendix 4 123
One Generation Shall Praise
Your Works to Another

About Truth78 131

ZEALOUS

*7 Commitments for the Discipleship
of the Next Generations*

What is Zeal and
Why Does it Matter?

DEEP DOWN, we wonder. We give them a Bible, teach them the truth, ask penetrating questions, lead them in prayer, affirm the good, confront the sin, provide a good example to follow, help them find good friends—but deep down we wonder if what we are doing is working.

They read the Bible and even memorize parts of it. They claim to believe the truth, give good answers to our questions, pray *the prayer*, do good things, admit their sin, follow our example, have good friends—but deep down we wonder if the fruit we are seeing will last.

We watch devoted, yet weary, parents faithfully bringing their children to church after a full week of family life, school, chores, social engagements, and endless activity to provide the best opportunities for their children to flourish in the life that is before them—and deep down we wonder if the Word of God that makes its way into the cracks of their busy lives will be enough to sustain their confidence in God and His Word.

We see young people rushing into youth group, wearing attire to fit in or to stand out, gathering for worship, singing songs of praise, and listening to the eternal words of life, while monitoring social media, thinking covetous thoughts about their friends' possessions, fearing rejection by those who have captured their hearts, and ignoring the one thing that will matter most in the last moment of their fleeting lives. Deep down we wonder if the Word of God that they're hearing and singing will penetrate their distracted hearts and conform them to the image of Christ.

We witness the tears and groanings of a Christian parent whose heart is broken over a child who has exchanged the truth he grew up with for the lies of the world.

We hear another parent weeping for a child who has forsaken the way that leads to life for a wider and brighter way that leads to destruction.

We observe bewildered parents who can hardly believe the words coming from the mouths of their offspring and the hard-hearted, God-defying attitudes and convictions that define their empty lives.

We listen to a dad speaking about his child who has married well and is raising delightful children, actively participating in church, flourishing in his profession, and doing all the good and right things he was taught to do, yet wondering if there is any evidence of saving faith.

Deep down we wonder if the children growing up in our homes, actively participating in our churches, and sitting in our classrooms will grow up to join the number of those who embrace Christ as their greatest treasure and passionately follow Him. Or will they instead join with those seeking treasure where it cannot be found, rejecting their only hope for everlasting joy?

We wonder if our children will be thriving in the way of infinite wisdom, or walking in the counsel of the wicked. Will they be joining the congregation of the righteous, or sitting in the seat of scoffers? Will they be like mighty oaks of righteousness sinking their roots deep into the life-giving streams of God's Word, or will they be like chaff nourished from the empty cisterns of the world and driven away by the wind of judgment? Will they stand in the freedom of Christ, or sink under the weight and condemnation of their unforgiven sin? Will they delight in the presence of the LORD, or dwell in everlasting darkness? Will they be forever singing praises to their Savior and King, or will they be forever weeping and gnashing their teeth with the ancient enemy of their souls?

For decades I have interacted with hundreds of Christian parents, children's ministry volunteers, youth leaders, teachers, pastors, grandparents, and ministry colleagues. Almost every one of them cares about the souls of the children growing up in their homes and churches. They want their children to trust in Christ, follow Him as

Lord, and obey His teaching. They desire nothing less for their children than everlasting joy and the fulfillment of all God's promises in their lives.

I have sensed, however, that not all of them were feeling an appropriate weight of responsibility for the souls of the children entrusted to them. Not all of them were paying close attention to the spiritual development of their children. Not all of them were taking the time to number their days of influence in the fleeting lives of their children. Not all of them were sensing the urgency of addressing the issues of a hardening heart.

Too many were lacking any plan for instructing their children in the truth. Too many were thinking that Sunday school was enough. Too many were believing that a Christian home was sufficient. Too many were assuming Christian friends offered adequate influence. Too many were consumed with other priorities at home and in the church. Too many were paralyzed by fear and overwhelmed by their parental circumstances without consistent support, wisdom, instruction, or encouragement. Too many seemed unconcerned about the absence of any appetite for the Word of God. Too many dismissed spiritually dangerous attitudes and behavior as "just a stage." Too many assumed it would all work out, and in the end their children would be fine. Too many were helping their children gain the world, while ignoring the threats against their soul.

Too many were lacking in zeal for the discipleship of the next generation. And zeal can make a significant difference.

▼ ▼ ▼

REASON FOR CONCERN

For more than 20 years, we've been hearing statistics and seeing disturbing trends indicating that between 50 and 90 percent of children growing up in the church no longer attend church after they leave home.[1] In 2003, George Barna not only provided data documenting the Church's decline

---

[1] For an overview of studies on young people leaving Christianity, including the range of estimates, see https://coldcasechristianity.com/writings/
are-young-people-really-leaving-christianity/

of spiritual impact on the next generation, but also offered principles and proactive strategies for responding to the concerns.

Some of what Barna recommended sounded promising. He said that millions of parents want a positive experience for their children in a nearby church with "a consistently high-quality ministry."[2] The potential of millions of members was enough to motivate many churches to increase their investment in children's and youth ministries. Bigger budgets and more staff held the promise of more children staying in church into adulthood. Quality programming does attract families to church. And many of those churches were motivated by the evangelistic potential to reach unbelieving families with the gospel. Unfortunately, the downward trends have continued because the emphasis was too often on quality programming, rather than on discipleship.

No amount of new programs could undo the pervasive spirit of indifference and "lackadaisical"[3] attitude in the church and among parents toward the spiritual development of children:

American parents—even those who are born-again churchgoers described by their church as "pillars"—are generally doing what their parents did with them: dropping off the kiddies at church and allowing the religious professionals to mastermind the spiritual development of the young people...adults tend to revert to what was modeled for them, noting that carting the kids to church and occasional religious events is sufficient. "After all" explained one mother, echoing a sentiment that has become a very common reply emerging from our research, "that's what my parents did with me and I turned out pretty good."[4]

Facts documenting the problem and proposed solutions have not improved the situation. If anything, the situation has gotten worse since Barna published his findings. One headline reporting on a recent Pew Research Study starkly stated: "In U.S., Decline of Christianity

[2] George Barna, *Transforming Children into Spiritual Champions: Why Children Should Be Your Church's #1 Priority* (Ventura, Calif: Regal Books, 2003), 40-41.
[3] Ibid., 42.
[4] Ibid., 78.

Continues at Rapid Pace."[5] Commenting on the study, Albert Mohler said, "Looking at the generation known as the Millennials, only 49% even described themselves as Christians. That's astoundingly low as compared to other recent American generations."[6]

The problem, it turns out, isn't lack of funds, but lack of biblical motivation. What the Church needs, and what parents need, is what the Bible commands—zeal.

ZEAL MATTERS TO GOD

From Genesis to Revelation, everything we are called to do in the service of our King, including the discipleship of the next generation, requires zeal. In Deuteronomy 6, Israel was given responsibility for the instruction (discipleship) of its children. The context for that instruction was zeal for God—"love the LORD your God with all your heart and with all your soul and with all your might" (6:5); zeal for His Word— "these words that I command you today shall be on your heart" (6:6); and zeal for discipleship—"teach them diligently to your children" (6:7).

In the New Testament, Paul appealed to his brothers and sisters in Rome to "present [their] bodies as a living sacrifice, holy and acceptable to God" (Romans 12:1). He then filled the next three chapters with exhortations that describe a living sacrifice that is holy and acceptable. That includes Romans 12:11 where Paul exhorts the Roman church, writing, "Do not be slothful in zeal, be fervent in spirit, serve the Lord." Zeal and fervency in serving the Lord matter because such is the service that is holy and acceptable to the Lord.

Zeal in Scripture is not simply enthusiasm. It is fervor and diligence born out of a passion for God and His glory. It is the result of a heart on fire for the glory of God that is uncontainable and spills out in zealous evangelism, discipleship, service, and good works.

The Lord hates the absence of zeal. We see that in His words to the church in Laodicea, "I know your works: you are neither cold

---

[5] "In U.S., Decline of Christianity Continues at Rapid Pace," https://www.pewforum. org/2019/10/17/in-u-s-decline-of-christianity-continues-at-rapid-pace/

[6] Albert Mohler notes that among Millennials, "The big factor...is the increase in those who do not attend [church] and the decrease in those who do." https://albertmohler. com/2019/10/22/briefing-10-22-19

nor hot. Would that you were either cold or hot! So, because you are lukewarm, and neither hot nor cold, I will spit you out of my mouth" (Revelation 3:15-16).

Throughout Scripture, God Himself is zealous to pass His truth on to the next generations. Our zeal is not only in keeping with God's will but, as we'll see in the chapters ahead, it is also following God's example.

7 COMMITMENTS FOR THE DISCIPLESHIP OF THE NEXT GENERATIONS

From what God has revealed in His Word and from what I've seen bear fruit in 40 years of ministry, I believe there are at least seven commitments that are essential for zealous discipleship of the next generation. The next seven chapters are dedicated to the fundamentals of those commitments.

I believe these seven commitments are critical, but they will be fruitless without zeal. For nearly three decades, I have been casting a vision for the discipleship of the next generations. Over the years, I have been part of a growing network of like-minded parents and church leaders across the country that I would describe as "having a vision for the next generation." I still believe vision is essential. It is one of the reasons we placed "Embrace a Biblical Vision" first in the list of seven commitments. It is often the place I start when coaching parents and church leaders. Certainly, the absence of vision in the church and home is a problem. However, I am now convinced that it is insufficient to have a vision—even a biblical vision—if it lacks zeal. A vision without zeal won't reverse the trends in the Church, and a vision without zeal rarely becomes reality.

ZEAL AND THE 7 COMMITMENTS

And yet, as much as zeal matters, as eager as I am to see the Church become more zealous for the discipleship of the next generation, and as concerned as I am by the pervasive neglect of this God-given responsibility, we can't *make* ourselves or anyone else zealous. Does this mean then that there is nothing we can do until we are zapped with zeal for the next generation? No. Even though zeal is ultimately a work of God in the heart, I believe there are things we can do that God will use to awaken zeal in us and in others.

In Colossians 1:28, Paul helps us understand our responsibility and our goal in discipleship: "Him [Christ] we proclaim, warning everyone [including our children] and teaching everyone [including our children] with all wisdom, that we may present everyone [including our children] mature in Christ."

In verse 29, we see the spirit in which we do that job and pursue that goal: "For this I toil, struggling with all his energy that he powerfully works within me." Paul labored to present everyone mature in Christ with energy that came from God. To the church in Corinth, Paul said that he "worked harder than any of them, though it was not I, but the grace that is with me" (1 Corinthians 15:10). Paul's zeal for serving the faith of others was the fruit of the zeal of the Lord at work in him.

This is not unlike our experience with faith. Faith is not the result of works; it is a gift of God (Ephesians 2:8-9), and yet we are called to "Fight the good fight of faith" (1 Timothy 6:12). Faith without works is dead, and we are to strive "for the holiness without which no one will see the Lord" (Hebrews 12:14).

Philippians 2:12-13 provides the key to understanding the relationship between that which only God can do and that which we must do—"work out your own salvation with fear and trembling, for it is God who works in you, both to will and to work for his good pleasure."

GROWING IN ZEAL

If you are persuaded by the importance of having zeal for the discipleship of the next generation but you're not yet sensing much zeal for this cause, then "work out" your zeal for the discipleship of the next generation, for God is at work in you both to will and to work for His good pleasure. And if His pleasure is for you to have this zeal—and I believe it is, given His own zeal for the discipleship of the next generation—then the zeal will come. This is why I commend embracing seven essential commitments and acting on them, trusting God not only for the grace to be able to act upon and to fulfill them, but also for the zeal without which your efforts will be unsustainable.

Let me illustrate how this works. Anyone leading a ministry for children and youth knows that recruiting volunteers to serve is a significant and challenging part of the job. By God's grace, I've recruited hundreds of volunteers over the years, many of whom were not particularly zealous about the discipleship of the next generations when they began their ministry (since people serve in next-generation ministry for many different reasons). As these men and women began the work of discipleship, however, I watched God ignite this zeal again and again in their hearts. It has been even more exciting to see what God does with that zeal: fresh ideas, new strategies, ministry expansion, energy, passion, prayerfulness, digging into the Word—all diligently aiming at true discipleship. Many are accomplishing more than I ever imagined and far surpassing me in zeal and commitment to the cause.

Like those first-time volunteers, I was not always zealous for this vision. Looking back, I can point to two things God used to ignite my zeal. First, in 1974, I was falling in love with a Christian Education major who was, and is to this day, more zealous for the discipleship of the next generation than anyone I have ever known. God has given Sally an unquenchable and very contagious zeal that He has used to ignite and sustain a zeal in me for more than four decades.

Second, in 1980, I was a 26-year-old follower of Christ who had the benefit of godly parents and other faithful servants of God who invested in my faith from Sunday school to seminary. Through those years, I grew in knowledge of God, love for Jesus, desire to spread the gospel, and passion to give my life in service to Christ. But in the middle of that year, God took me to the church of a new young pastor, John Piper. Thus began what would be more than 33 years under the consistent influence of his faithful expository preaching and biblical teaching.

God used John Piper's preaching to open my eyes to dimensions of God that I had never seen before. The roots of my faith grew deeper into truths I had not grasped before. I was being shaped by a growing knowledge of God's Word and God's glory by God's grace through a man who still has a zeal for the truth and for the glory of God and for spreading that zeal for the joy of others. His zeal was contagious. Over the next decade, Sally and I experienced a rising, irresistible, and persistent zeal to spread the knowledge of this glorious God and the life-giving truth from His Word to the next generation.

ZEAL ACCORDING TO KNOWLEDGE

If we are not shaped by a true knowledge of God, we may be zealous, but not for what will save the next generation. In Romans 10:1-2, Paul writes, "my heart's desire and prayer to God for them is that they may be saved. For I bear them witness that they have a zeal for God, but not according to knowledge."

In preaching on this text, John Piper said:

> There's a zeal that is not a saving zeal and there's a zeal that is part of being saved...one is not according to knowledge and the other is according to knowledge...if [Paul's] beloved kinsmen that [he] wants so badly to be saved, are not saved because their zeal doesn't accord with knowledge, then knowledge is massively important.[7]

Piper then applies it to the next generation:

> This is really, really important. If you care about raising kids, you're going to bring your kids up to have that knowledge or not. If you're a pastor, it matters. If you're a Sunday school teacher, it matters. If you're a small group leader, it matters. If you're a seminary teacher, it matters. There is a zeal that doesn't accord with knowledge. Oh, they get all kinds of knowledge, and it's leading them straight to hell.[8]

ZEAL FOR OUR CHILDREN'S CHILDREN'S CHILDREN

Our labors have a far-reaching effect on generations that we will never know. When Psalm 78:5 speaks of declaring the "testimony" to the "next generation," at least three generations are specified, two of which did not yet exist. In this psalm, we read that the fathers were commanded to teach their children so "that the next generation might know them, the children yet unborn [the unborn grandchildren of these *fathers*], and arise and tell them to their children [the unborn

---

[7] John Piper, "Zeal for God: Deadly or Indispensable?" a sermon delivered at Kenwood Baptist Church, Cincinnati, Ohio. October 10, 2013. https://www.desiringgod.org/messages/zeal-for-god-deadly-or-indispensable
[8] Ibid.

great grandchildren of these *fathers*], so that [those unborn children will] set their hope in God and not forget the works of God" (verses 5- 7).

One generation declaring the truth about God to the next is a pattern established by God. God makes Himself known in other ways, but He has ordained this as one of His primary means for making His glory known to all generations. Knowing that your influence will reach far beyond the children born in your lifetime is a powerful motivator for zeal.

ZEAL FOR STRONG FAITH
IN A WORLD OF HOSTILITY

Zeal for the discipleship of the next generation is also intensified by the desire to prepare children for a world that is increasingly hostile to the truth of God's Word. This should not surprise us. Jesus warned His disciples in Luke 21:17, "You will be hated by all for my name's sake," and in verse 16 He promises, "some of you they will put to death." In John 15:19, Jesus explains why: "If you were of the world, the world would love you as its own; but because you are not of the world, but I chose you out of the world, therefore the world hates you."

Almost to His last breath, Jesus was thoughtfully and purposefully preparing His disciples for a world that would hate them. If we are His disciples, those words are for us, too. The urgent, earnest desire to prepare just as thoughtfully and purposefully the children who are facing, or will face, these challenges fuels our zeal.

ZEAL FOR DUTY AND DELIGHT

As followers of Christ, we have a duty to pass on to our children the truth that has been entrusted to us. But duty alone can be drudgery, and it rarely helps us persevere when we are discouraged, overwhelmed, and frustrated in our efforts. Discipleship of the next generation is *more* than duty. Investing our time, talents, and resources in the faith of our children and grandchildren is investing in their joy, and not only their joy but ours as well. Since Christ endured the cross by keeping His eyes on the joy that was before Him (Hebrews 12:2), keeping our eyes on the joy that is before us and our children will enable us to endure the ups and downs of our discipleship efforts.

The Apostle John declared that he had "no greater joy than to hear that [his] children are walking in the truth" (3 John 1:4). What news of your children or grandchildren would be your *greatest* joy? That they made the soccer team? That they graduated with honors? That they got accepted to Yale? Our world presses us to prioritize anything and everything but that which will truly satisfy. There is no greater joy in this life, or the next, than being reconciled through Christ to God:

> You make known to me the path of life; in your presence there is fullness of joy; at your right hand are pleasures forevermore (Psalm 16:11).

As we experience this joy in God, our joy will overflow into the discipleship of the children in our homes and churches. The next generation will be best served by parents and teachers who have a joy-fueled, contagious vision for their lives.

WE WONDER

It's good to wonder about the next generation—to think soberly about what's ahead for the children in our homes, our churches, and our communities.

But we don't have to wonder in fear.

We don't have to wonder if our efforts will be in vain. We can set our hope in God, trusting in the goodness of His sovereign will. If we're zealous and resolved to do what God has instructed, if we're hoping in a glorious God, then we can wonder what work of discipleship God might be pleased to do in our hearts, our homes, our churches, our communities, and beyond.

If we pray earnestly for zeal for the discipleship of the next generation, we can wonder in hope.

Seven
Commitments

▼ ▼ ▼

1

Embrace a Biblical
Vision for the Faith of
the Next Generation

I WANT TO INTRODUCE you to two hypothetical pastors named Pastor Program and Pastor Vision.[9] Both of these men are serving solid, gospel-preaching, evangelical churches. Both of them are leading churches that are growing and thriving. I have a lot in common with them theologically and enjoy spending time with both of them. Both of them are burdened for the lost people in their communities, and both have a strong desire to grow their churches through evangelism. Though they may look the same, upon closer inspection, they're not.

Pastor Program believes that ministry to children and youth is one of his church's highest priorities, as reflected in the number of staff and budget dollars that the church has committed to this priority. He discovered a long time ago that this ministry is important to people, especially

---

[9] I am calling them *pastor* even though they don't necessarily have to be pastors in order to represent the two kinds of leaders I have in mind.

parents, when they are considering a church. "If children have a good time and look forward to coming to church," he said, "then their parents will be more inclined to come themselves." He has never forgotten the church growth advice he received 30 years ago from an elder in his first church who told him, "Pastor, if you give the kids something fun to do, the parents will flock to you."

Pastor Vision also believes that ministry to children and youth is one of his church's highest priorities, as reflected in the number of staff and budget dollars the church committed to this priority. The leadership in his church understands that children and youth are included in their biblical responsibility as elders to "shepherd the flock of God that is among [them]" (1 Peter 5:2). He never forgot the advice he received 30 years ago from an elder in his first church who said "tending to the faith of children and youth in this church is as important as tending to the faith of their parents." Ever since, Pastor Vision has taught his people that the biblical responsibility they have to serve one another; to build each other up; to bear one another's burdens; to care, comfort, encourage, exhort, reprove, rebuke, equip, instruct; and to stir up one another to love and good works applies as much to children and youth as it does to adults.

Pastor Program takes next-generation ministry seriously. He knows that there are many things that are competing for the attention of young people. He is concerned that this generation will be lost if the Church doesn't stay up-to-date. He encourages children's and youth ministry leaders to apply cutting-edge technologies and educational philosophy to all of their programs. He often tells them, "Kids are too important to bore them with outdated, old-fashioned methodologies. When children and youth have fun at church, positive attitudes about church are formed that will stay with them the rest of their lives. These positive experiences will help motivate them to come to church as adults. Furthermore, because habits are formed early in life, those who regularly attend church when they are young will likely continue attending as adults."

Pastor Vision takes next-generation ministry seriously. He knows that there are many things competing for the attention and affections of young people. He wants to do all he can to make sure those growing up in his church will be treasuring Christ as their eternal hope 20, 40, 80 years from now, with eyes looking to God for all they need, hearts overflowing in praise to the Lord, and lips declaring His infinite worth. He prays for their faith to be so firmly established that they will endure, faithful to the end, be able to stand in the day of judgment, and delight in the presence of the Lord forever. He knows that lifetime attitudes and convictions are formed early in life, so he inspires the young people in his church to delight in God and form a radical God-centered orientation to all of life. He wants them to be ignited with a contagious, lifelong passion for the supremacy of God in all things for the joy of all people through Jesus Christ.

Rather than boring children by repeating simple truths and shallow presentations of the Bible, he wants the children growing up in his church to taste the joy of mining the depths of the Bible and discovering wonderful things from God's Word. He encourages parents and children's ministry leaders to give careful attention to what the children are learning and to apply methods that will be effective in establishing a solid biblical and doctrinal foundation for children and youth that can sustain them throughout their lives.

Pastor Program's church has a great website that advertises "a well-equipped nursery, Sunday school for all ages, and a wide range of activities for children and youth, including children's choirs beginning at kindergarten."

Pastor Vision's church has a great website that advertises "a well-equipped nursery, Sunday school for all ages, and a wide range of activities for children and youth, including children's choirs beginning at kindergarten"—all of which are shaped by a five-point vision that they will be mighty men and women of faith who:

- have a big view of God who rules the universe and who upholds the universe by the word of His power.
- love the Word and learn to live by it, developing a faith that is able to stand even in the hard times.
- are radically committed to seeing the gospel proclaimed throughout the world for the glory of God and the joy of all peoples.

- desire and know how to effectively fight sin—forsaking the idols of this world and laying claim to an inheritance that far surpasses the temporal comforts that idols claim to offer.
- be parents who love each other, are equipped to lead their children to God, and are encouraged and supported as they strive to nurture the faith of their children.

It is my hope and earnest prayer that there will be an increasing number of leaders in the Church who think like Pastor Vision, because activities and games alone will not prepare children for the suffering—or the successes—of life ahead of them. The Church needs leaders who are persuaded that the discipleship of children growing up in Christian homes and churches should be shaped and oriented around a biblical vision for the next generation.

DOING VERSUS LEADING

Many young people growing up in Christian homes participate in "activity-oriented" programs in the church. Such programs focus on providing activities for children and youth that are not clearly linked to any goal or purpose (vision). An activity-oriented ministry puts more emphasis on the present, and less, if any at all, on the future. They concentrate more on what they are doing with the children, and less on where they are leading the children.

Though Pastor Vision offers the same "well-equipped nursery, Sunday school for all ages, and a wide range of activities for children and youth" as Pastor Program, Pastor Vision identifies the specific purpose and goal for each activity beyond caring for children and giving them (and their parents) a positive experience. A vision-oriented program or activity is clearly linked to specific discipleship goals that are fueled by prayer and the desire for children to whole-heartedly embrace Christ.

Vision-oriented parents, Christian educators, and church leaders think about and act according to what they want to be true of their children 10, 20, and 40 years hence. Their priorities are shaped by asking questions like:

- What do we want our children to know and understand about God and His Word?
- What do we want them to understand about the gospel?
- What marks of faith and spiritual maturity do we want them to have?
- What portions of the Bible do we want them to be able to quote from memory by the time they graduate from high school?
- What kind of husband and father, or wife and mother do we want them to be?
- What do we want them to teach their children?
- How would we want them to respond when tragedy strikes or when they face suffering in their lives?
- What will fortify them against the temptations of wealth, pleasure, and success?
- What do we want them to be trusting in when they are taking their last breath?

ARROWS AND BUILDINGS

Psalm 127:3-5 and 1 Corinthians 3:9-17 offer two images that reinforce vision-oriented discipleship. In Psalm 127:4, the psalmist describes children as "arrows in the hand of a warrior." Although not necessarily the main point, this image does suggest that the "warrior" has a target in view. Just as arrows are intended to be aimed at something, so our discipleship of children should have a specific aim or goal in view. Vision-oriented leadership in the church must first be able to define the target, and then be able to inspire parents, children's and youth ministry staff, volunteers, church leaders, and the congregation as a whole to direct their efforts toward the target. Without a target, those who are investing in the next generation are pointing their "arrows" in various directions and, at times, even in competing directions. Sometimes the "arrows" are just aimlessly pointed and are shifted when a new idea or whim surfaces. Consequently, little or no discipleship progress is ever made.

In 1 Corinthians 3:9-17, the Apostle Paul says God's people (including the next generations) are "God's building" (verse 9) being built on the foundation of Jesus Christ. Paul and Apollos saw themselves as builders on that foundation.

Before construction on a building can begin, it is best to have a detailed vision for what that building will be. This vision must be shared with everyone who is working on the building so that the vision and ultimate purpose for the building will be fulfilled. The most skilled builders, the most experienced contractors, and the finest craftsmen who have the best tools and state-of-the-art equipment cannot successfully build a building without a detailed vision and a commitment from everyone involved to work toward the same goal. Likewise, the most effective and fruitful discipleship activity in our homes and churches will be governed by a biblical vision that is shared by all who are contributing to the discipleship effort.

ACTIVITY SHOULD SERVE VISION

Psalm 78:1-8 beautifully illustrates this relationship between activity and vision. Verse 4 identifies the activity, namely telling the coming generations "the glorious deeds of the LORD, and his might, and the wonders he has done." There are many good reasons someone might tell stories about the glorious deeds of the LORD to children in Sunday school. Children love hearing stories. And we can be glad when they are happily engaged for more than an hour in meaningful activity, enjoy the time they spend at church, and are eager to come back for more. But this is not the main reason Psalm 78 gives for declaring the LORD's glorious deeds. The value of stories about the glorious deeds of the LORD is not their entertainment value but their power to lead children to "set their hope in God" (verse 7). The vision-oriented ministry leader wants much more than a good time and meaningful engagement for children. He will not rest until the children in his care "set their hope in God," remember "the works of God," and "keep his commandments." Psalm 78:7 unites our discipleship *activity* around a clearly stated *vision* for our children. It also ignites a passion for that vision.

Our children are growing up in a world of distractions that threaten to lure their affections away from God and His glorious deeds. We tremble at the thought of them being blinded by empty promises and exchanging the truth about God for a lie. Our passion for a generation of men and women who are setting their hope in God is ignited by an intense desire for their everlasting joy and a serious concern for their souls. We are desperate for our children to count everything as loss for the surpassing worth of knowing Christ. We don't want them being duped into trusting in the worthless idols of this age and selling their souls for what cannot satisfy or save. This Psalm 78:7 vision forms the desire of our hearts for our children that fuels our zeal for their discipleship.

IGNITE ZEAL FOR THE VISION

Without igniting zeal, a well-crafted vision statement for the discipleship of the next generation ends up being just another well-crafted vision statement. It does not inspire the kind of passion that can motivate and sustain the efforts of a disciple-making parent and teacher. How do you ignite that zeal for the next generation?

1. Ground your vision for the next generation in the Word of God. We, as God's image-bearers, are wired by our Creator to respond to His purposes, His priorities, His desires, and His Word. When our vision is grounded in the Bible, and when we use biblical language to express that vision, it resonates in the hearts of God's people and prompts a response from the heart that says, "Amen!" and "Yes! That's what I want for my children!" Of course, there are hundreds of verses that can help define and express our vision, including these four examples:

> ### That Our Children Will Fear God and Walk in All His Ways
> "And now, Israel, what does the LORD your God require of you, but to fear the LORD your God, to walk in all his ways, to love him, to serve the LORD your God with all your heart and with all your soul" (Deuteronomy 10:12).

> ### That Our Children Will Have a Deep and Abiding Love for Christ
> "Abide in me, and I in you. As the branch cannot bear fruit by itself, unless it abides in the vine, neither can you, unless you abide in me. I am the vine; you are the branches. Whoever

abides in me and I in him, he it is that bears much fruit, for apart from me you can do nothing. If anyone does not abide in me he is thrown away like a branch and withers; and the branches are gathered, thrown into the fire, and burned" (John 15:4-6).

That Our Children Will Have a Big View of God, Who Works in All Things to Accomplish His Purposes

"...I am God, and there is no other; I am God, and there is none like me, declaring the end from the beginning and from ancient times things not yet done, saying, 'My counsel shall stand, and I will accomplish all my purpose,' calling a bird of prey from the east, the man of my counsel from a far country. I have spoken, and I will bring it to pass; I have purposed, and I will do it" (Isaiah 46:9b-11).

That Our Children Will Learn to Rightly Handle the Word of Truth

Do your best to present yourself to God as one approved, a worker who has no need to be ashamed, rightly handling the word of truth (2 Timothy 2:15).

2. Remind them that suffering is coming. On a Sunday morning in the spring of 2002, Pastor John Piper prepared to preach a message from Roman 8:18-25 entitled, "Subjected to Futility in Hope." He opened with a prayer that included these words:

Lord, put a rock of hope under the feet of this congregation, I pray, so that when the winds of pain and suffering and groaning and decay blow, we will not lose our footing. Use these six magnificent statements of hope in this text to sink our roots down in and around the granite truth of your promises so that our leaves will not wither in the drought which is coming for everyone in this room sooner or later.

As Piper began the introduction to that message, he said:

> Just so you know what's in my pastoral mind here, I'm getting you ready
> to die. I'm getting you ready to suffer. I'm getting you ready to know
> what I'm thinkin' when I come to your hospital room…so that I don't
> have to preach and I can just hug you.[10]

This prayer and desire of my pastor's heart challenged me to keep
sinking my own roots into the "granite truth" for whatever challenges
are coming my way. They also helped to express my own heart and
vision for the next generation.

The Apostle Peter tells us in 1 Peter 1:6-7 that trials of various
kinds test the "genuineness" of our faith. These trials are coming for
me and you, and for the children in our families, and in our churches.
When the inevitable troubles come, we want them to be deeply rooted
in the granite truth of the promises of God. We want them to have
a rock-solid faith that remains steadfast and proves genuine so that
in those moments of grief, marital problems, miscarriage, wayward
children, disability, cancer, hostility, persecution, or whatever trouble
may come their way in life, we don't have to preach, we can just hug.

**3. Use language that is meaningful to the particular people you want
to motivate and inspire.** Tailoring your words to the shared experiences of the people in your church body can be a great help to
fueling zeal. For example, because we drew from Pastor John's phras-
ing at Bethlehem Baptist Church, the congregation knew exactly
what we meant when we said we wanted our children to become,

> coronary Christians who go hard after God and who live by faith in
> future grace; who declare God's glory with undistracting excellence,
> gutsy guilt, and broken-hearted boldness; and who are devoted to

---

[10] John Piper, "Subjected to Futility in Hope—Part 2, Romans 8:18-25," a sermon
delivered at Bethlehem Baptist Church, Minneapolis, Minn. May 5, 2002.
https://www.desiringgod.org/messages/subjected-to-futility-in-hope-part-2

spreading a passion for the supremacy of God in all things for the joy
of all peoples through Jesus Christ...[11]

Many of these familiar phrases had an emotional impact that sparked
zeal for the next generation. I was personally impacted by the series of
sermons that helped me understand what it means to "live by faith in
future grace." After that series, I could say to a group of parents who
had been similarly impacted, "Let's raise a generation that is living
by faith in future grace," and it would prompt hearty affirmation.
The phrase reminded them of a truth that was meaningful to them,
which sparked a zeal for it to be meaningful to their children as well.

4. *Keep eternity in view*. Moses prayed in Psalm 90:12, "teach us to
number our days." There is wisdom in numbering the days of our
children as well. Realize that within a vapor of time each child will
be standing before the King of kings and Lord of lords and will hear
one of two declarations from the Judge of all the earth. Our children
will either hear:

"Well done, good and faithful servant...Enter into the joy of your master"
(Matthew 25:21).

Or they will hear:

"You wicked and slothful servant!...cast the worthless servant into the
outer darkness. In that place there will be weeping and gnashing of
teeth" (Matthew 25:26, 30).

The burden of this reality informs my priorities for parenting, grand-
parenting, and ministry, and it feeds my zeal for the discipleship of
my children, grandchildren, and the children of my church.

---

[11] Some of the vision language that was formed in the context of Bethlehem's ministry
has worked well outside of that church. I have included in the Appendix the vision
statement formed at Bethlehem that carried over to my ministry at College Park
Church of Indianapolis, Indiana.

John Angell James (1785-1859) had a 50-year ministry as a British pastor that was marked by significant zeal for the discipleship of the next generation and a concern for souls in light of eternity. In a challenge for parents to take their responsibility seriously, James trembled as a father as he pondered the eternal implications of his efforts:

> My child is immortal, and his eternal destiny in great measure depends upon me. I am not only the author of his existence—but in some measure of his destiny. I shall be the means perhaps of raising him to heaven, or sinking him to perdition. I am educating him to be an associate with the devil and his demons in everlasting fire, or a companion with the innumerable company of angels in everlasting glory. O God, help me! for who is sufficient for these things? [12]

The ultimate vision for our children is for them to be companions with the "company of angels in everlasting glory." Who, indeed, is sufficient for such things? May God Himself help us to embrace a biblical vision for the faith of the next generation.

SUMMARY

Having a vision is crucial for discipleship of children and youth. Vision-oriented leaders consider where they are going—clarifying their goals—and then they carefully develop and implement an intentional plan to pursue those goals. By having a long-term vision, leaders can more effectively develop a discipleship strategy that evaluates every program, activity, curriculum, and resource in terms of the greater vision.

Looking Ahead: *Where is this vision applied? Who bears the responsibility for this vision of discipleship?*

---

[12] John Angell James, "Earnestness implies a deep sense of the tremendous responsibility of the parental relation" in *The Church in Earnest*, chapter 5, section III (Boston, Mass.: Gould, Kendall, & Lincoln, 1849), 116-117.

COMMITMENT

2

Foster a Robust Partnership Between Church and Home

THE JOHNSON FAMILY is seen every Sunday at Grace Bible Church. The parents, both raised in non-Christian homes, are grateful for the solid biblical instruction their children receive in Sunday school and various other children's and youth programs. They feel a weight of responsibility lifted from their shoulders, knowing that men and women with more biblical knowledge and maturity are caring for the spiritual needs of their children. Once the children are dropped off at their classrooms, Mr. and Mrs. Johnson enter the corporate worship service to enjoy undistracted time of being spiritually fed. Amidst all the busyness of life and the challenges of parenting in an increasingly secular age, the Johnsons look more and more to their church to meet the spiritual needs of their children.

The Willis family is also seen every Sunday at church, faithfully sitting in the same pew in the sanctuary. It's readily apparent that the four Willis children are fully engaged in the service—singing along, heads bowed during prayer, and actively taking notes during the sermon. This is not by accident. The parents take the discipleship of their children very seriously. Participating in the corporate worship service together as a family is a high priority. But the Willis's believe that the weekly worship service is merely a tiny investment in their children's spiritual development. At home, Mr. Willis leads the family in daily devotions, and biblical instruction is prominently featured in their studies at home. However, there is one place in the church where you will never find the Willis children—Sunday school or any other children's and youth programming. They have assumed almost total and exclusive responsibility for discipling their children.

Here are two sets of parents who love their children deeply and long for their children to know, trust, and love Jesus. Yet, each set of parents is failing to fully see and understand an important responsibility and means of grace God has designed for their children's discipleship. The church is not primary, and the parents are not sufficient.

WHO IS RESPONSIBLE FOR THE DISCIPLESHIP OF THE NEXT GENERATION?

The scenario involving these two families captures a reality that exists in many churches to one degree or another. It often creates a tension that centers on the question of who is responsible for the discipleship of the next generation. There are extremes on either side. Some say the church is solely responsible for the spiritual education and development of children. Others believe that responsibility rests entirely with parents, and it is wrong for the church to step in where only parents belong. In their view, the only biblically warranted involvement the church should have is to exhort, instruct, and equip parents to fulfill their God-given responsibility.

Most parents and church leaders who have wrestled with this issue usually find themselves somewhere between these two extremes, tilting one direction or another.[13] In many cases, the responsibility that the church and parents have for the spiritual development of

---

[13] For further reading on this topic, see Timothy Paul Jones' helpful book, *Perspectives on Family Ministry: Three Views* (Nashville, Tenn.: B&H, 2009).

children is ambiguous. How the home and church should relate and carry out this responsibility is seldom taught or discussed.

Sometimes parents assume their children are being discipled through the ministries of the church more than what is actually the case. Sometimes church leaders assume more is happening at home than is actually the case. In many cases, neither parents nor church leaders are giving much thought to the discipleship of the children, and even less thought to the nature of their responsibility.

Where there is a decline in the intentional, comprehensive discipleship at home and in the church, we shouldn't be surprised to see a corresponding rise in biblical illiteracy for those who have grown up in these homes and churches.

Paul identified the problem centuries ago when he asked, "how are they to believe in him of whom they have never heard?" (Romans 10:14). How are they to believe without any functional knowledge or understanding of the Word of God? Though it breaks our hearts to see it happening, it should not surprise us to see increasing numbers of children forsaking Christ and His Church after they leave home and enter a world where they find little encouragement to ever darken the door of the church again.

A reversal in this disturbing trend will require utter dependence on the grace of God, and both church and home picking up the mantle of responsibility they share for the discipleship of their children. In an effort to impress this responsibility on parents, British Pastor John Angell James in 1849 urged parents to remind themselves often of their responsibility for the souls of their children:

> You will, if you are [thoughtful will], often say, "I am a parent. I am a Christian parent. I profess to believe my child has a soul, the salvation or the loss of which will depend much upon me. Yes, upon me does it much depend whether my children are to be forever in glory, or in [Hell]. How inexpressibly solemn! How tremendously important! I have not only bodies to care for, or minds to cultivate—but souls, immortal souls, to bring to Christ! Every other parent, whether beast or bird, by instinct teaches its offspring the highest good of which their nature is capable; and

shall I, by neglecting to [disciple my children], neglect the highest good on which their [eternal hope rests]? Even the sea monsters nurse their young—and shall I be more cruel than they?"[14]

For us to do better than "sea monsters" at home and in the church, it needs to be broadly understood and embraced that the church and the home (family) are the two institutions established by God for the discipleship of the next generation. Both parents and church leadership must assume this privilege and responsibility with faithfulness and accountability to God. Then, as this second commitment suggests, they must foster a robust partnership between church and home.

Before considering what this involves, let's consider the biblical justification for this partnership.

A BIBLICAL PATTERN

Probably the clearest instruction given to parents is in Ephesians 6:4 where fathers are exhorted to bring their children "up in the discipline and instruction of the Lord." Moses, undoubtedly, had parents in mind in Deuteronomy 6 when he instructs Israel to "diligently" teach their children "these words that I command you today" (verse 6). We can clearly see that the context for this instruction is the home when Moses continues instructing them to "talk of them ["the words"] when you sit in your house, and when you walk by the way, and when you lie down and when you rise" (verse 7).

Throughout the book of Proverbs, parental responsibility for instruction of children is assumed. In Proverbs 1:8 we read, "Hear, my son, your father's instruction, and forsake not your mother's teaching," and in Proverbs 6:20 we read, "My son, keep your father's commandment, and forsake not your mother's teaching."

---

[14] John Angell James, "Earnestness implies a deep sense of the tremendous responsibility of the parental relation" in *The Church in Earnest*, chapter 5, section III (Boston, Mass.: Gould, Kendall, & Lincoln, 1849), 115-116. (Note: The brackets in this quote indicate where I have substituted a few words to more plainly communicate James' thoughts to a contemporary audience.)

Paul's words in 2 Timothy 1:5 and 3:15 imply that Eunice and Lois taught their young son and grandson, and it can be assumed that it was these women of sincere faith who first acquainted Timothy with "the sacred writings" that he had known from childhood.

The Bible has even more to say about the corporate responsibility that the people of God have for the instruction of the next generation. Moses clearly had parents in mind when he spoke the words recorded in Deuteronomy 6:4-7, but because he was addressing all of Israel at the time (Deuteronomy 1:1), we should assume that he was also placing the responsibility on the whole congregation.

In Psalm 78, we see this corporate responsibility stated more clearly. In verse 3, Asaph speaks of truths "that our fathers have told us," and in the next verse he resolves not to hide these truths "from their children, but tell to *the coming generation* the glorious deeds of the LORD." It seems that Asaph is reinforcing the congregation's responsibility to instruct "their children."

Verse 5 of Psalm 78 points again to the individual responsibility that "our fathers" had to teach their children. Following that statement, Asaph expresses the corporate desire in Israel for the next generation to know the truth so that they would rise up and teach "the children yet unborn...so that they should set their hope in God" (verses 6-7). Clearly, every person in Israel needed to understand his and her individual responsibility for the instruction (discipleship) of the next generation and to share with the whole congregation the responsibility to make "the testimony" (verse 5) known to all generations.

The New Testament teaches that the Church is responsible for discipleship, and there is nothing to suggest that children should be excluded. To the Colossian church, Paul says, "Him we proclaim, warning *everyone* and teaching *everyone* with all wisdom, that we may present *everyone* mature in Christ" (Colossians 1:28).

To the Ephesians he writes, "he gave the apostles, the prophets, the evangelists, the shepherds and teachers, to equip the saints for the work of ministry, for building up the body of Christ, until we all attain to the unity of the faith and of the knowledge of the Son of God...to the measure of the stature of the fullness of Christ, so that we may no longer be children... rather...we are to grow up in every way...into Christ" (Ephesians 4:11-15).

In 2 Timothy 2:2 Paul reminds his disciple, "what you have heard from me in the presence of many witnesses, entrust these to faithful men, who will be able to teach others also." When we read Hebrews 10:24, "let us consider how to stir up one another to love and good works," children should be part of our consideration. When we are told earlier in that letter to "exhort one another every day, as long as it is called 'today,' that none of you may be hardened by the deceitfulness of sin" (Hebrews 3:13), it would seem that "none" includes young ones and old ones alike.

Our zeal for the discipleship of the next generation must be characterized by the weight of biblical, God-given responsibility. Not only every parent, pastor, elder, youth leader and Sunday school teacher, but also every follower of Christ should feel the weight of this responsibility and an obligation to help young people become and grow as disciples.

Together, the church and home can accomplish more for the discipleship of the next generation than what could be done by either institution alone. Each brings influence and resources the other does not have. Thus, focusing on the powerful impact their partnership can have is vital.

THE CHURCH AND DISCIPLESHIP

Churches are ideally suited for casting a biblical vision for the next generation that the whole congregation and every parent in the church can embrace. The church can promote the vision through preaching and teaching. It provides a corporate worship service that cannot be duplicated in the home. It is also well-suited for the formation of a structured discipleship plan for children and youth.

Another important role that the church plays in partnership with the home is to provide a community of support, encouragement, inspiration, and accountability for both the "disciple" and the "discipler." Young parents have the benefit of Titus 2-type relationships with seasoned parents who can provide counsel and practical wisdom gleaned from years of experience. There is also the potential benefit for children and youth to learn and be influenced by other adults who share a common faith, vision, and values with their parents.

Children also have the opportunity to grow in faith alongside other young people in church who are learning the same things and being encouraged in the same direction. One of the keys to the effective and fruitful discipleship of the next generation at home and in the church is an effective and fruitful ministry to men. The influence that a husband and father has on the strength of a marriage, the stability of the home, and the physical, emotional, and spiritual development of children is incalculable. The investment that a church makes helping men understand their role and responsibility as shepherds of their home and giving them the tools and support they need, can bear fruit in the lives of their children and grandchildren for generations.

PARENTS AND DISCIPLESHIP

Even though there is more I could say about the unique opportunities the Church has for impacting the faith of the next generation, I'll conclude this chapter by considering the crucial role parents have in the discipleship process.

It almost goes without saying that parental opportunities for impact and influence on an individual child abound. The bond between a parent and child, unlike that of any other relationship in our lives, is a tremendous asset for the discipleship of the next generation. As parents, we have a particular and unique interest, affection, accountability, and responsibility for our own children. Because of this unique relationship, we will be more committed and more invested in the physical, emotional, and spiritual development of our children than anyone else on the planet.

Among the significant assets that parents bring to the church-home partnership is knowledge. No Sunday school teacher or youth worker has the opportunity to know an individual child like a parent does. Parents are able to see strengths and weaknesses, evidence of grace, and evidence of depravity and sin. They will witness spiritual growth in a child's life and know where growth is needed.

Parents also have time and significantly more access to the children. In most cases, school-aged children whose families are active in the church will spend less than four hours weekly in the discipleship activities of the church. Those few hours can be very impactful but certainly cannot offer the everyday experiences of life in which the Word of God can be tested, tried, and found to be true. Rarely are there opportunities within that short window of time when a young person can be challenged to trust God in a specific situation and take a step of faith. Parents have these opportunities daily! Every day the Holy Spirit puts children in situations where, with the guidance and influence of their parents, they can apply truth that they have learned and see God at work in their lives.

Parents are in a position to provide life-long discipleship for their children as they grow from infancy to adulthood and move through the various seasons of life. A parent's discipleship influence will likely extend not only to their children and to their children's children, but to all generations.

Once again, Pastor John Angell James provides a fitting note to strike at the end of this chapter. Even though these words were written to young men, his point reinforces for all of us the generational influence of our actions:

> Consider then, the family relationships you will sustain. Look on and anticipate what kind of husband, father, master and tradesman, you are likely to make; and how you shall preside over the domestic economy. Some woman's destiny for life will hang upon you, and the happiness of a family, perhaps a numerous one; and then upon their conduct will depend, by an onward succession, the destiny of others to descend from them. You will thus commence a dark or a bright line of human existence, which will run onward through all future generations, and be still going forward when the last trump shall sound. Misery or bliss, at the distance of centuries...may be traced back to you.[15]

As we faithfully foster a robust partnership between church and home, may God be pleased to make a "bright line of human existence" run from those who labor faithfully together for the discipleship and

---

[15] John Angell James, *Addresses to Young Men: A Young Man's Friend and Guide* (Morgan, Penn.: Soli Deo Gloria Publications, 1995. Originally published in 1860), 32.

everlasting joy to "all future generations, and be still going forward when the last trump shall sound!"

SUMMARY

God has called both the church and home to raise up the next generations to know, honor, and treasure God through Jesus Christ. This is accomplished through a strategic, loving partnership between the church and home. This partnership affirms that parents by proximity, opportunity, and God's design, bear a unique responsibility for nurturing their children's faith. (See Deuteronomy 6:4-7.) This partnership also affirms the role and responsibility of church leadership to provide encouragement and training for parents, as well as the formal instruction for children and youth.

Looking Ahead: *What specifically, is this generation of parents and teachers to teach the next generation?*

3

Teach the Breadth
and Depth of the
Whole Counsel of God

THE FIRST MORNING Suresh Singh visited Sunday school with his friends, the teacher told the Exodus story. Suresh had never heard about God leading the people of Israel out of Egypt with signs and wonders. The next week, the teacher taught the same story again. And the next week. And the next.

"I heard the Exodus story there every week for *two* years because they didn't have anything else," Suresh recalls. One of the main reasons Suresh didn't learn more of the Bible in that time was because his village in Manipur, India didn't have any curriculum for children available in its language (even though the Bible had been translated in Hmar 26 years before).

You would never see a church in North America repeating the Exodus story to children for two years, but I am concerned that churches with access to a wealth of resources for teaching the Bible to children don't give them much more than a slice of that Bible.

Often, young children are repeatedly told the same stories, while vast portions of Scripture are overlooked. By the time most children in Christian families are five years old, they have heard the story of "Noah and the Ark" dozens of times, while other significant portions of the Bible have been ignored. If "all Scripture is breathed out by God and profitable for teaching, for reproof, for correction, for training in righteousness" (2 Timothy 3:16), shouldn't we acquaint children with as much Scripture as they can absorb? Rather than boring them with shallow presentations of the same stories repeatedly, shouldn't we broaden the foundation of their biblical knowledge?

When we limit the Scripture children are exposed to, we also limit their view of God. God needs to be seen in the vast array of His multifaceted character. How can the faithfulness of God to His chosen people be understood outside the context of numerous stories of God's dealings with unfaithful Israel? How can children understand that God's promises are true unless they are given the end of the matter where God's promises come to fruition? Only through exposure to a variety of stories and biblical passages can children understand the balance of God's character—that He is merciful, yet just; that God is high and lofty, and yet He dwells in intimate fellowship with His people.

NOT SHRINKING FROM DECLARING
THE WHOLE COUNSEL OF GOD

Few verses in the Bible make me tremble more than Acts 20:26-27. There we find these staggering words that Paul spoke to the Ephesian elders: "Therefore I testify to you this day I am innocent of the blood of all, for I did not shrink from declaring to you the whole counsel of God." Pondering the implications of this verse is enough to keep any pastor, parent, or teacher awake at night.

We know from Moses' instruction to Israel in Deuteronomy 6:6-7 that "these words" should be on our hearts, and we should "teach them diligently" to our children. We know from Psalm 78:5 that God "established a testimony in Jacob and appointed a law in Israel," which we have been commanded to teach to our children. We know from Paul's words in 2 Timothy 1:14 that we have been entrusted with a "good deposit" that must be "guarded."

All of these texts reinforce the responsibility we have and fuel our zeal to faithfully impart the truth of God's Word to the next generations. However, the parting words of the Apostle Paul to his fellow-elders on the shores of Miletus make us realize just how weighty the responsibility is. Paul understood that he was accountable for declaring the "whole counsel of God" to these men. Neglecting to do so would make him guilty of their blood. Two chapters earlier, Luke records Paul's response to the Jews in Corinth when "they opposed and reviled him" for testifying that "the Christ was Jesus." Paul "shook out his garments and said to them, 'Your blood be on your own heads! I am innocent'" (Acts 18:5-6).

The idea that we could be guilty of someone's blood for neglecting our responsibility to impart what has been entrusted to us has its roots in God's word to the prophet in Ezekiel 3:17-21 and 33:1-9. Ezekiel's responsibility was likened to a watchman on the wall, whose responsibility it was to be alert and warn those inside the wall if he saw "the sword coming." If his neglect of that responsibility resulted in the death of those he was charged to warn of imminent danger, their blood would be on his head. However, if people died because they failed to heed the warning of a watchman who faithfully discharged his duties, he would be innocent, and the blood of the people would be on their own heads.

No doubt Eliza Spurgeon understood her place on the wall for the sake of her children, including her firstborn, Charles, who never forgot her prayer:

Now Lord, if my children go on in their sins, it will not be from ignorance that they perish, and my soul must bear swift witness against them at the day of judgment if they lay not hold of Christ.[16]

We have been entrusted with God's counsel and with the responsibility to faithfully impart it to the next generations. We are not liable for how children respond, but we will bring judgment upon ourselves if our children perish in ignorance because we have neglected our responsibility for their instruction in the whole counsel of God.

---

[16] Charles Spurgeon, *Charles Spurgeon Autobiography, Volume 1, The Early Years* (Carlise, Penn.: The Banner of Truth Trust, 1962), 44.

WHAT IS THE WHOLE COUNSEL OF GOD?

Coming to terms with this responsibility begs us to consider what the "whole counsel of God" actually is. How else can we ever say with confidence that we have faithfully imparted to our children the truth that has been entrusted to us and, therefore, are innocent of their blood? Answering this question is important and has been challenging as parents charged with the responsibility to bring up our two daughters in the discipline and instruction of the Lord. As a pastor, it has been even more important and challenging to answer this question for parents and the church as a whole in an effort to equip them to faithfully carry out the calling and responsibility to the children entrusted to them.

The easy way to answer the question is to hold up a Bible and say, "This is the whole counsel of God." Even though this is easy, it is not especially helpful when we must decide specifically what to teach and when to teach it. Paul spent about two years with the Ephesian elders—what was the scope and sequence of his teaching? The Bible is filled with truth that could take a lifetime to understand, and even longer to effectively impart it all to the next generation. How can we begin to know what comprises the whole counsel of God so that we can have the confidence that we have sufficiently declared it?

BREADTH AND DEPTH

A good place to begin is to first impress upon parents and church leaders that there is both a breadth and a depth to the counsel of God as it is revealed in the Scriptures. For example, we must give the next generation a broad knowledge of God's goodness, love, mercy, faithfulness, justice, power, compassion, happiness, and holiness, along with other numerous attributes of God. But there is also depth to each of those attributes that our children must begin to grasp.

Take God's love, for example. Most Sunday school children learn very early that God is love and that He loves them. Fewer of those children will ever get beneath the surface to understand the true essence and depth of God's love. We are often too satisfied at home and in our churches when our children learn that God loves them without that love being fully explored, defined, or given a context within God's holy nature. Paul could not be satisfied with the Ephesian believers having such an anemic understanding of God's love. "For this reason" Paul bowed his "knees before the Father, from whom every family in heaven and earth is named," that they "may have strength to comprehend with all the saints what is the breadth and length and height and depth, and to know the love of Christ that surpasses knowledge" (Ephesians 3:14-15, 18-19). The same can be said about our knowledge of God's power. Two chapters earlier, Paul told this same group of saints in Ephesus of his unceasing prayers for several specific things, including that they would know "the immeasurable greatness of [God's] power toward us who believe" (Ephesians 1:18-19).

Notice in both instances Paul suggests that we can fathom neither the depth of His love "that surpasses knowledge" nor His "immeasurable" power. If we are responsible to declare the whole counsel of God, how can we have confidence that we have succeeded if the limits of His love and power cannot be comprehended or measured? What seems impossible for adults to comprehend can seem even more challenging when we seek to teach these truths to our children.

My initial response is simply to challenge us to care about what we are teaching, and especially what we are not teaching our children. If readers come to the end of this chapter feeling the weight of the responsibility to raise their children in truth, if they are motivated to take steps to faithfully and intentionally help the next generation to know as much of the breadth and depth of God's counsel, if alongside these intentional efforts they join us in seeking the "Spirit of truth... to guide [our children] into all the truth" (John 16:13), I am confident our children will be beneficiaries of the breadth and depth of God's counsel, and we will be innocent of their blood.

THE WHOLE COUNSEL OF GOD IN FIVE CATEGORIES

In discerning what is an intentional and faithful effort to teach the whole counsel of God to our children, it can be helpful to think in terms of the following five categories:

1. *Bible Survey and Book Studies*—Begin in the preschool years by giving children a chronological, story-based presentation of the truth. This will introduce them to the key people, places, events, and themes of the Bible. Along the way, it is important to emphasize God as the author and main character in each of those stories and certainly of the Bible as a whole. This will provide children a fundamental Bible foundation upon which the other truth will stand. Once children can see the breadth of God's Word as it has been revealed, then it is helpful to look more deeply into the individual books of the Bible as the children grow.

2. Biblical Theology deals with the overarching storyline of Scripture, whereby God progressively reveals His redemptive purposes, which come to their complete fulfillment in the Person and work of Jesus Christ. The aim is for the student to discover how the Bible's many diverse stories, written over time, all serve to communicate one main, unified message. Children need to see how the various themes in Scripture all connect to Christ and His work of salvation.

3. Systematic Theology is a topical approach to teaching the foundational doctrines of the Christian faith. Systematic theology presents the Bible's teaching on various subjects, one at a time, and summarizes each topic based on the entirety of Scripture.

4. Gospel Proclamation is an explicit and comprehensive presentation of the essential truths of the gospel, leading to a clear understanding of the Person and work of Jesus Christ and what it means to respond in true repentance and faith.

5. Moral and Ethical Instruction acquaints students with the nature, role, and importance of God's laws and commands, the wisdom literature, and the moral and ethical teachings of Jesus and the apostles. This instruction is necessary for understanding God's character and standards and our need for the gospel, along with guiding believers in righteous and godly conduct.

Keeping these five categories in mind helps to guide us as we consider the scope and sequence of our instruction, and can provide us with the appropriate breadth and depth of Scripture needed to faithfully instruct our children in the whole counsel of God.

Don Carson's words regarding the full counsel of God can be a helpful summarizing guide in determining whether our teaching encompasses the breadth and depth Paul has in mind:

What he must mean is that he taught the burden of the whole of God's revelation, the balance of things, leaving nothing out that was of primary importance, never ducking the hard bits, helping believers to grasp the whole counsel of God that they themselves would become better equipped to read their Bibles intelligently, comprehensively.[17]

SUMMARY

This generation is to teach the next generation the whole counsel of God—a core knowledge of the breadth and depth of Scripture that is essential for coming to salvation in Christ and living a life of faith. Teaching the whole counsel includes five categories that address specific and essential questions: Bible Survey and Book Studies (What's in the Bible? Who is the Bible about?), Biblical Theology (What's the main message of the Bible?), Systematic Theology (What are the essential doctrines of the Christian faith?), Gospel Proclamation (What do we need to be saved? How are we saved?), and Moral and Ethical Instruction (How are we to live?).

Looking Ahead: *What is critical for proclaiming the gospel within our teaching of the whole counsel of God?*

---

[17] D. A. Carson, "Challenges for the Twenty-First-Century Pulpit" in *Preach the Word: Essays on Expository Preaching: In Honor of R. Kent Hughes* (Wheaton, Ill: Crossway Books, 2007), 177-178.

4

Proclaim the Glorious Gospel of Jesus Christ

IMAGINE WITH ME the following scene. It's a beautiful Sunday morning at Somewhere Bible Church. Graham Johnson, along with his wife, Karen, are gathered in a small conference room with 14-year-old Ethan, who is obviously a little nervous.

The Johnsons have known Ethan all his life. Mrs. Johnson and Ethan's mom are good friends. Mr. Johnson is "cool," but he's also an elder, and this meeting is a little weird. Ethan is not sure what to expect.

Ethan is a great kid. He is well-behaved at church and at home. He excels in school, has a good group of friends, and is well-liked by his teachers. A few months ago, he expressed a desire to be baptized. Ethan didn't realize it meant having to be interviewed by an elder.

He is glad to see Trevor Gilmore there. Trevor is the small group leader for ninth-grade boys, and he led the baptism class that Ethan attended.

Ethan noticeably relaxes as a casual conversation begins about his favorite sport. The three adults are obviously amazed as Ethan spouts off batting averages for several players and the season wins and losses for the two teams he is expecting to be in this year's World Series. Looking at his watch, Graham Johnson smiles and shifts into interview mode. After Trevor prays, the conversation continues:

Mr. Johnson: Ethan, would you mind sharing with us how you became a Christian?

Ethan: Well, a long time ago when I was seven years old, my grandma died. One night around that time I was thinking about her. I wondered about what she was doing. I wondered what it was like to be dead. I wondered if I would really go to heaven when I died. I got really scared and went downstairs to talk with my mom and dad. My dad shared with me how I could be sure I would go to heaven when I die. My mom and dad showed me some verses like John 3:16 and shared the gospel with me. Then we prayed, and I asked Jesus into my heart.

Mr. Johnson: Thank you, Ethan. From what your dad shared with you that night and from the things you have been learning in Sunday school and small group, what do you understand about the gospel?

Ethan: Well, the Bible says that because we are all sinners we can't go to heaven. But Jesus died for our sins, so if we believe in Him and ask Him into our hearts we can go to heaven when we die.

Mr. Johnson: I see. So what does it mean to believe in Jesus?

Ethan: Uh...well...you have to believe that Jesus died for your sins...and...uh...that He's the Son of God?

Mr. Johnson: Yes, that's right. The Bible teaches that Jesus is the Son of God and that He died for our sins. Do you think Satan believes that Jesus is the Son of God and that He died for our sins?

Ethan: Uh...yes...maybe.

Mr. Johnson: Because Satan believes in Jesus, do you think Satan will go to heaven?

Ethan: No, definitely not!

Mr. Johnson: Ethan, why do you think sin keeps us from going to heaven?

Ethan: Uh...uh...I'm not sure.

Mr. Johnson: That's okay, Ethan. Whatever the reason, you know that sin is a problem, and it keeps us from going to heaven when we die.

Ethan: Yes, that's right!

Mr. Johnson: You said that it is important for us to believe that Jesus died for our sins. That's so true, and I am very glad you believe it. So how do you think Jesus' death solves our sin problem?

Ethan: Well...when Jesus died, He took our sins...and died for them so that we don't have to...

Let's step out as Ethan and Mr. Johnson continue their conversation...

BREADTH AND DEPTH OF THE GOSPEL

Serving as a pastor and elder in two different churches for more than three decades, I have had the privilege of hearing hundreds of testimonies from people who were preparing for baptism or church membership. A number of them have been young people in settings and interactions similar to the one just described. In each case, the goal is to discern a credible profession of faith and a sufficient understanding of the gospel. In some cases, like the one we just observed, such discernment can be difficult to achieve.

How can a young man grow up in a Christian home, attend a gospel-preaching church all his life, hardly ever miss a Sunday school class or youth meeting, and at 14 years old have such a deficient understanding of the only reality that will matter to him in a thousand years? As disappointing as a conversation like this can be, it is even worse when the person being interviewed is twice Ethan's age, or perhaps is even one of his parents.

Ethan clearly had picked up some bits and pieces of gospel truth, but obviously there had been no successful effort to help him understand the breadth and depth of the gospel. To be clear, being able to demonstrate a solid understanding of the gospel does not define a true believer, just as a weak understanding of the truth does not necessarily indicate an absence of genuine faith. The question is, how can anyone confidently embrace the gospel and confess faith in the saving work of Christ if he really doesn't understand it? How can we (or our children) have any assurance that we are born again if we don't understand the basis for our assurance? Should we be baptizing children who are eager to "get dunked" when they are functionally ignorant about the significance of that external expression of a glorious internal and eternal work of Christ in the life of a believer?

This fourth commitment—Proclaim the Glorious Gospel of Jesus Christ—was born out of the earnest desire for those growing up in our churches and all who come after them to inherit a robust understanding of the gospel "so that they should set their hope in God and not forget the works of God" (Psalm 78:7). This hope in God was secured in the perfect life, death, and resurrection of His Son, our Lord Jesus Christ. This hope is the hope of the gospel. This gospel hope proclaims to desperate sinners that salvation is by grace alone, through faith alone, in Christ alone!

But it's important to understand that the gospel is shaped and defined by essential doctrines found throughout Scripture. For example, all of God's attributes including His triune nature are reflected in the gospel message. Man's nature, the fall, God's covenants with His people, the law and other essential truths progressively revealed in the Old Testament are also key to understanding the gospel.

Therefore, we must be careful that our priority to communicate the gospel does not compromise our commitment to teach the breadth and depth of the whole counsel of God. Yes, it is important that the Old Testament be understood and taught with the gospel in view. However, in recent years there has been an overemphasis on explicitly linking every Bible lesson to Jesus and the gospel. This topic came up in a recorded interview I had with John Piper, who raised an important concern about turning this perspective into a type of simplistic interpretative formula. He said:

> The danger in making a beeline to the cross too quickly and too methodically and regularly is, number one, it'll start to sound artificial. It'll start to sound monotonous. It'll start to be fanciful, because you'll come up with really clever ways of doing things that aren't really there and it'll keep you from seeing important things that are there.[18]

There is a time and place for presenting children and youth with a step-by-step summation of the gospel. But our greater goal is to lay a solid gospel foundation for our children by acquainting them "with the sacred writings, which are able to make you wise for salvation through faith in Christ Jesus. All Scripture is breathed out by God and profitable for teaching, for reproof, for correction, and for training in righteousness, that the man of God may be complete, equipped for every good work" (2 Timothy 3:15-17). As we faithfully instruct our children in the truth, may God make them wise for salvation and alive in the hope of the gospel.

ESSENTIAL TRUTHS

Gospel-focused discipleship begins with an understanding of the essential truths of the gospel:

---

[18] John Piper, interview quoted in "Does Every Lesson Need to be a 'Jesus and the Cross' Lesson?" August 1, 2018. https://www.truth78.org/blog/post/every-lesson-a-jesus-lesson/

1. God is the sovereign Creator of all things.

Implication ▾ God made you. You belong to God. God is your ruler.

2. God created people for His glory.

Implication ▾ God created you to know, trust, and love Him most of all.

3. God is holy and righteous.

Implication ▾ God's commands are holy and righteous. You must obey God's commands all the time.

4. Man is sinful.

Implication ▾ You have disobeyed God's commands. You are a sinner.

5. God is just and is right to punish sin.

Implication ▾ You deserve God's punishment of death and hell. You are helpless to save yourself.

6. God is merciful. He is kind to undeserving sinners.

Implication ▾ You must depend on God's mercy in order to be saved.

7. Jesus is God's holy and righteous Son.

Implication ▾ Jesus came into the world to save you.

8. God put the punishment of sinners on Jesus, so that His righteousness might be put on them.

Implication ▾ Jesus died on the cross to be punished in your place.

9. God offers the free gift of salvation to those who repent and believe in Jesus.

Implication ▾ God tells you to believe in Jesus and repent of your sins and you will be saved.

10. *Those who trust in Jesus will live to please Him and will receive the promise of eternal life—enjoying God forever in heaven.*
Implication ▾ If you are trusting in Jesus for your salvation, you must follow Him. Jesus has promised that when you die He will bring you to heaven to live with and enjoy God forever.[19]

GOSPEL LIVING

This understanding of the essential truths, by God's grace, must lead to a necessary response of true repentance and belief in Christ alone.

Gospel-focused discipleship must lead to gospel living, which includes walking according to the Spirit (Romans 8: 4), denying our selfish desires and living for Jesus (Luke 9:23), daily trusting Him, (Matthew 6:25-34), submitting to His will and His ways (James 4:7), depending on the guidance and strength of the Holy Spirit (Psalm 32:8; Zechariah 4:6), putting sin to death (Colossians 3:5-9), growing in holiness (2 Corinthians 3:18), and honoring and treasuring Christ above all (Colossians 2:2-3).

GOD'S SOVEREIGN WORK

We have been entrusted with a glorious message. Embracing that message is the only hope the next generations have for their salvation and everlasting joy. As effective as we are in helping our children understand and believe the whole message of the gospel in all of its fullness and depth, we mustn't forget that the application of the gospel to the souls of our children takes a miracle that we cannot perform.

Our children are born dead in their trespasses and sins. The most God-centered, gospel-focused curriculum and the most well-funded, age-appropriate, parent-integrated program in the world cannot raise our children from spiritual death. Neither can it turn hearts of stone into hearts of flesh (Ezekiel 11:19).

Ultimately, the salvation of children is in God's hands. Jesus tells us that, "No one can come to me unless the Father who sent me draws him" (John 6:44). God is completely sovereign and chooses whom He

[19] See Appendix 3: 10 Essential Gospel Truths.

wills (Exodus 33:19b). Unless God is at work in a child's heart, all our efforts are in vain (Luke 18:27).

Yet, our efforts are often the very means by which God in His providence accomplishes His saving work. As we faithfully proclaim the glorious gospel of Jesus Christ, we labor with all our hearts, prayerfully and consistently guiding, inspiring, and exhorting the next generations toward a personal and sincere response to the gospel that bears the fruit of love, trust, and delight in God through Jesus Christ. May God be pleased to bring about the Spirit-wrought, grace-dependent transformation that we so zealously desire for the next generation.

SUMMARY

The gospel is simple yet amazingly profound, freely offered yet extremely costly, and should be communicated as such. While the gospel can be simply conveyed to children, our approach should not be simplistic. We are to lay a solid, deep foundation by clearly and patiently presenting the key essential truths of the gospel found throughout the Bible. Through repeating and explaining these with increasing depth, we hope to help children see the splendor, majesty, and holiness of God, the enormity of their sin problem, and the immeasurable love and grace of God in Christ, resulting in true repentance and genuine belief.

Looking Ahead: *How do we teach in a way that will encourage faith?*

5

Disciple the Mind, Heart, and Will

IT'S NOT ENOUGH for children just to know what the Bible says and teaches. Crucial for the fruitful discipleship of the next generation is the opportunity to instruct the mind, engage the heart, and influence the will. Consider how my wife addressed the mind, heart, and will while teaching a boy who told a fish tale.

Sally was teaching a class of sixth graders from Psalm 32, a lesson with the theme "from brokenness to forgiveness." Through underlining words in the text, defining words, asking and answering questions, and following the reasoning in the passage, the students discovered the truths that covering up sin creates misery and is harmful, but sincerely confessing sin brings forgiveness. The teaching had instructed their minds.

But knowledge alone does not bring freedom from sin. Repentance does. And for that to happen, the heart must be engaged and the will influenced. As Sally taught the lesson, pondering and praying how to reach their hearts, she was prompted to ask if anyone had covered up sin and what the result was of hiding that sin.

One boy raised his hand and confessed that he had been in a fishing contest. He had lied and said he caught three fish when in fact he had caught two. This "three-fish catch" had resulted in a trophy. The students sat in stunned silence listening to this testimony of honest confession.

"What has been the result of hiding this sin?" my wife asked.

The young man quietly replied, "Every time I look at that trophy, I feel guilty." It was a sobering moment in the classroom.

Sally explained to the class that feeling guilty is a blessing that can lead us to repentance. Together, the class discussed how to be free from sin through confession, and by the end of the class the boy understood what steps he needed to take to be free from the guilt of his sin. Not only did he understand what to do—his mind had been informed; but he wanted to be free from his sin—his heart had been engaged.

Yet he was not free until he took the step of confessing his sin to his parents, and then confessing it to God and asking for forgiveness. At that point, the will was engaged. The child had acted on the truth.

Though we do not always see the result of our teaching—the informing of the mind with truth—we must help children understand how to apply the truth to their own lives. If they own that truth, embracing it in their hearts, the Holy Spirit will bring opportunities to act on the truth, engaging the will.

Sometimes parents and teachers emphasize one dimension at the expense of the others, to the detriment of the child. For example:

- If we concentrate on conforming the will to God's standard of behavior without paying attention to the heart beneath the behavior, children will tend toward a faithless self-righteousness, instead of depending on Christ's righteousness.
- If we emphasize the heart but neglect instructing the mind, we can ignite and fuel feelings that, while genuine, are not in conformity to God's nature or will.
- If we stress instructing the mind, but give little attention to how God's Word is to be responded to, acted upon, and lived out, we risk giving children the impression that God and His Word are irrelevant to their lives.

Mind, heart, and will—all three are essential. How then can you reach them?

1. INSTRUCT THE MIND.

By God's design, biblical instruction begins by addressing the mind. Consider how Scripture repeatedly uses words, such as: teach, declare, instruct, acquaint, tell, etc. In response to God's Word, we are called to pay attention, know, think about, consider, meditate, etc. This goes beyond merely reading Scripture and providing biblical information to our children—although that is an important first step.

Consider these words from John Piper in his article, "A Compelling Reason for Rigorous Training of the Mind":

> I was reading and meditating on the book of Hebrews recently, when it hit me forcefully that a basic and compelling reason for education—the rigorous training of the mind—is so that a person can read the Bible with understanding.

> ...The issue of earning a living is not nearly so important as whether the next generation has direct access to the meaning of the Word of God. We need an education that puts the highest premium under God on knowing the meaning of God's Book, and growing in the abilities that will unlock its riches for a lifetime. It would be better to starve for lack of food than to fail to grasp the meaning of the book of Romans. Lord, let us not fail the next generation![20]

Instructing the mind involves training and equipping the next generations to "unlock" the riches of the Word of God. By necessity, it must involve teaching them to interact and engage with the Bible itself. One of the most telling indicators of the state of Christian education in our churches is the increasing absence of the Bible in Sunday classes. And, if children do have Bibles, they are rarely

---

[20] John Piper, "A Compelling Reason for Rigorous Training of the Mind," July 13, 2005. https://www.desiringgod.org/articles/a-compelling-reason-for-rigorous-training-of-the-mind

called upon to interact with and carefully study a text—learning to observe, ask specific questions, analyze, summarize, compare, etc. Rather, an emphasis on "hands-on active learning" (physical activity) has replaced active instruction of the mind. This begs the question: When our children and students reach adulthood, will they know how to read, study, and interpret the Bible, "rightly handling the word of truth" (2 Timothy 2:15)? Will they be able to biblically answer the "hard" questions like, "Why is there suffering and evil in the world?" Will they have the critical thinking skills necessary to articulate and defend God's truth in a hostile culture?

There is no substitute for biblical instruction of the mind. It must be a priority and is as crucial to discipleship as one leg is to the proverbial three-legged stool. If any one of the legs is missing, the stool collapses. The challenge before us is great and won't be accomplished if we give in to intellectual laziness in our homes and churches. Sunday school classes filled with fun activities, light-hearted lessons, and feel-good relational engagement cannot bring about the renewal of the mind that comes from reading and studying God's Word.

Christian faithfulness requires the development of the believer's intellectual capacities," writes Albert Mohler, "in order that we may understand the Christian faith, develop habits of Christian thought, form intuitions that are based upon biblical truth, and live in faithfulness to all that Christ teaches. This is no easy task, to be sure. Just as Christian discipleship requires growth and development, intellectual faithfulness requires a lifetime of devoted study, consecrated thinking, and analytical reflection.[21]

2. ENGAGE THE HEART.

Children with Christian parents can grow up in church, be familiar with the Bible, have all the right answers, and yet be in spiritually mortal danger because they have never loved the truth or the Author of the truth. They risk being like the very knowledgeable Pharisees, about

---

[21] Albert Mohler, "The Glory of God and the Life of the Mind," November 12, 2010. https://albertmohler.com/2010/11/12/the-glory-of-god-and-the-life-of-the-mind/

whom Jesus said, "This people honors me with their lips, but their heart is far from me; in vain do they worship me" (Matthew 15:8-9). John Piper offers a corrective vision:

> What we want from the next generation is not just heads full of right facts about the works of God; we want heads full of right facts and hearts that burn with the fire of love for the God of those facts—hearts that will sell everything to follow Jesus into the hardest places of the world.[22]

Knowledge of God, His work, and His ways will not save unless it engages the heart and brings about right desires and affections. Yet, as the late British Pastor Martyn Lloyd-Jones explains, the response of the heart is dependent on first knowing the truth:

> Truth comes to the mind and to the understanding enlightened by the Holy Spirit. Then having seen the truth the Christian loves it. It moves his heart...as you see the glorious truth about the love of Christ you will want it, you will desire it. So the heart is engaged.[23]

This movement from head to heart is ultimately the work of God; however, God's Spirit is often pleased to accomplish that work through parents and teachers who not only instruct the mind but also engage the heart of the child. First and most importantly, we must guide, implore, and encourage them to whole-heartedly trust Christ.

"If they are to be partakers of eternal life, they must trust in this Jesus Christ who saves," writes Tedd Tripp. "Our children must receive Him, turn to Him, hold fast to Him, and rest in Him alone for salvation. Ultimately, the work of the Holy Spirit must transform our children into people who rest in Christ alone for salvation. Our

---

[22] John Piper, "One Generation Shall Praise Your Works to Another," March 19, 2000. https://www.desiringgod.org/messages/one-generation-shall-praise-your-works-to-another
[23] Martyn Lloyd-Jones, *Spiritual Depression: Its Causes and Cures* (Grand Rapids: Eerdmans Publishing Company, 1965), 61.

role is to bring them the gospel and urge them to embrace Christ the Savior."[24]

This intentional heart engagement is crucial both before and beyond conversion. To briefly touch upon this topic, I would like to suggest four basic principles to guide our efforts in engaging the hearts of our children.[25]

1. Ask questions that help children to understand the true condition of their heart.

For example, after reading a verse such as Romans 3:23, "for all have sinned and fall short of the glory of God," you might ask questions like, "Is this true of you also? What evidence is there in your own thoughts, feelings, words, and actions that this is true? What is the consequence of sin? Can you fix this? Who alone can help you?"

2. Help children connect biblical truth to real-life situations they experience.

Children and youth do not readily see or understand how the truth of God's Word applies to their lives. They need to be shown that the Bible is relevant and authoritative to every aspect of life. One of the reasons why parents are indispensable for the discipleship of children is because they have significantly more opportunities to apply the truth to real-life situations.

For example, a child learns "The name of the LORD is a strong tower; the righteous man runs into it and is safe" (Proverbs 18:10) without knowing how to personally apply it in his life. A parent may notice fearfulness in his or her child. The parent can now use this situation to talk about and help the child apply Proverbs 18:10 by explaining that God is like a strong tower—almighty and unshakable—providing a sure refuge to all who run to Jesus. God wants us to call upon Him in prayer whenever we feel afraid.

---

[24] Tedd Tripp, "A Child's Call to Conversion: Faith as a Christian Mark," October 1, 2010. https://www.ligonier.org/learn/articles/childs-call-conversion-faith-christian-mark/
[25] See Appendix 1 for resources that can provide a more thorough treatment of this topic and practical strategies for this second discipleship priority.

3. Encourage children to actively interact
with and respond to the truth.

Telling children the truth and getting them to verbally affirm it does not necessarily mean they are comprehending, agreeing with, or internalizing it. By asking specific types of questions of a text, you can guide them to personally respond. For example, in reading the parable of lost son from Luke 15, you could ask questions such as, "Are you like either son at times? Are the things of this world giving you greater treasure, joy, and excitement than God? Do you think that as long as you behave a certain way—being outwardly good—that you will be acceptable to God?"

4. Guide children in seeing what heart desires
and affections God commands.

Rather than asking how they "feel" regarding a particular text or biblical truth, show them what desires and affections God commands in response; for example, "repent and believe the gospel" (Mark 1:15); "Delight yourself in the LORD" (Psalm 37:4); "Trust in the LORD with all your heart, and do not lean on your own understanding" (Proverbs 3:5); "Humble yourselves before the Lord" (James 4:10).

3. INFLUENCE THE WILL.

David sings in Psalm 40:8, "I delight to do your will, O my God; your law is within my heart." Paul tells us in Romans 2:13, "For it is not the hearers of the law who are righteous before God, but the doers of the law who will be justified." James exhorts us in James 1:22, "be doers of the word, and not hearers only, deceiving yourselves." In John 14:15, Jesus says, "If you love me you will keep my commandments." And in verse 21, Jesus says, "Whoever has my commandments and keeps them, he it is who loves me."

The evidence of true saving faith is a growing desire to walk in obedience to Christ. While this is dependent on the transforming work of the Holy Spirit, God also expects His children to exert real effort—submitting and conforming their wills to His perfect will. We cannot bring about this grace-wrought, Spirit-empowered transformation in the lives of our children. However, we can lead them to pray and ask God to change their hearts, making them "doers of the word" and not just "hearers." In our teaching and in discussing the Word with young people, we need to encourage a biblical response to the truth they have heard. With a view toward them developing the heart and will of a disciple, we show them what response the Word of God requires of them, and encourage them to step out in faith. Our role as parents and teachers is to challenge, encourage, and inspire children to follow Jesus, walk in His ways, and "fight the fight of faith" every day of their lives.

Here are a few ways we can influence the will toward submission and obedience to God:

1. Impress upon them God's sovereign authority over their lives.
Children must understand that God is their sovereign Creator. He made them and owns them. We all must answer to Him—believer and unbeliever alike. Even before conversion, children must be trained to recognize and rightly respond to authority, beginning with their parents' authority. When you teach a two-year-old to obey Daddy and Mommy in picking up his toys, you are giving him a precursor to godly submission and obedience that, Lord willing, will serve him in true godliness when he reaches adulthood.

2. Emphasize the authority of Scripture.
All of our thoughts, feelings, words, and actions must submit to God's Word. For example, when teaching a verse such as Ephesians 6:1, "Children, obey your parents in the Lord, for this is right," ask questions such as, "Is God asking you to obey just when you feel like it? Is He saying to obey only when it seems fair?" Highlight the biblical meaning of commands in Scripture.

3. Help them see that Scripture addresses all of our words and actions.
Too often young people do not see and understand the sufficiency and relevance of Scripture in responding to everyday situations.

For example, Philippians 2:4 says, "Let each of you look not only to his own interests, but also to the interests of others." How does this address a schoolmate who is having a hard time with his math homework? Suppose your sibling really wants to play a certain game but you want to play another? What if grandma needs help cleaning her house but you want to go to the park with friends?

4. Guide them to see that submission to Christ and obedience to His Word is for their joy.
In reference to God's commands David says, "Moreover, by them is your servant warned; in keeping them there is great reward" (Psalm 19:11). God's commands and our submission to them are not meant to squash our joy but to enable and increase it.

5. Encourage them to see and employ the help God has provided.
God has provided His children with everything we need to help us grow in conformity to Christ (2 Peter 1:3)—most importantly God's Word, the indwelling power of the Holy Spirit, and prayer. But parents, the church, and other godly believers are there to help children grow in godliness.

6. Help them see that submission and obedience is a life-long, grace-dependent endeavor.
Acknowledge that following Jesus and growing in obedience is a slow, steady progression. It involves daily fighting sin in our lives, stepping out in faith, trusting Jesus in new situations, and obeying specific commands. But we still will fail time and time again. Ultimately, our hope is in Christ and His perfect obedience. He graciously extends forgiveness when we confess our sins and turn to Him.

Our discipleship efforts must challenge, encourage, and inspire children to "work out [their] own salvation with fear and trembling," according to the knowledge that they have been given, trusting that God will awaken the desire of their hearts to then act on what they know, "for it is God who works in [them] both to will and to work" [the impossible] "for his good pleasure" (Philippians 2:12-13).

One final, vitally important thought regarding discipling the mind, heart, and will: As parents and teachers, we must model these life-giving truths. Reaching the heart of the child begins with the heart of the parent and teacher. Remember the order of discipleship that Moses outlined for Israel in Deuteronomy 6:6-7. First, "these words that I command you today shall be on your heart." Then, "teach them to your children."

"Teaching our children the truth is absolutely necessary, but it is not sufficient," writes Randy Alcorn. "The solid foundation for a life is not just hearing the words of God, but doing them (Matthew 7:24-27)." He continues:

> By our own example as their parents, we must teach our children God's truth, demonstrating it in application and obedience. The truth that time must be spent with God must be demonstrated by the time we spend with God. The truth about Christ's forgiveness must be shown as we seek and grant forgiveness in our home. The truth that evangelism is important must be demonstrated by our efforts in evangelism. As parents, we must model our stated convictions with courage and devotion. Otherwise what we do will speak so loudly they won't hear a word we're saying. Sometimes our children will fail to listen to us. Seldom will they fail to imitate us.[26]

SUMMARY

For children to personally know, embrace, and apply biblical truth, we need to disciple the mind, heart, and will. Toward that end, we must diligently instruct the mind, providing them with the proper tools and skills needed to rightly read, study, interpret, and apply Scripture.

While fully acknowledging that only God can bring Spirit-wrought, grace-dependent faith in Jesus, and lead us to walk as His faithful disciples, it is our responsibility to engage the heart—to guide, inspire,

---

[26] Randy Alcorn, "Training Our Children," August 11, 1992. https://www.epm.org/resources/1992/Aug/11/training-our-children/#ixzz3JTkNY8yu

and implore children toward a personal and sincere response to God's truth. Finally, true saving faith will be evidenced by a growing desire to walk in obedience to God. While this is dependent on the work of the Holy Spirit, God does expect His children to exert effort, choosing daily to trust Christ, submit to Him, and follow in obedience. Therefore, we guide, challenge, and encourage students to specific Christ-like thoughts, words, and actions.

Looking Ahead: *We can fulfill all the commitments covered so far—embrace a biblical vision, build a robust partnership between church and home, teach the whole counsel of God, proclaim the glorious gospel of Jesus, and disciple mind, heart, and will—and still have children fail to set their hope in God. What more can we do?*

6

Pray with Dependence on God's Sovereign Grace

IN 1982, AND AGAIN in 1985, Sally and I stood before our brothers and sisters in Christ, a new baby in our arms, and made five promises in a special service of dedication. Since then, I have led hundreds of parents in two churches for nearly three decades in making those same promises. The last of the five includes the following:

> Do you promise, *God helping you, to make it your regular prayer, that by God's grace* your children will come to trust in Jesus Christ alone for the forgiveness of their sins and for the fulfillment of all His promises to them, even eternal life, and in this faith follow Jesus as Lord and obey His teachings?

There is nothing Christian parents should want more for their child than eternal life and everlasting joy in the presence of Jesus Christ. Even if, tragically, that were not our greatest desire for our children, we cannot escape the God-given responsibility we have as parents and church leaders to faithfully raise our children in the hope of the gospel. Neither can we escape the reality that our children will only be saved by the grace of God through faith in Jesus Christ (Ephesians 2:8). It is a sobering and humbling reality that I (along with every other parent) am absolutely incapable of giving my children what my heart desires most for them.

Even when we are zealous for the discipleship of the next generation, we are woefully unequal to the task before us. Our best efforts have no power to raise our children from spiritual death to everlasting life. We cannot turn hearts of stone into hearts of flesh. We cannot create in them the desire and the will to follow Jesus and walk in His ways. We cannot remove the sin that keeps them eternally separated from God. The most biblical vision, the best parenting strategies, and the most comprehensive Deuteronomy 6:7-9 instruction in the Christian faith do not guarantee that children will be born again and that their parents will experience the joy of seeing them walking in the truth (3 John 1:4).

This is why the fifth promise we made as new parents included the indispensable clause: "God helping you, to make it your regular prayer that by God's grace..."

Leading children to salvation is only possible with God's help and the transforming power of His grace (Luke 18:27). The most important thing I can do to provide what I desire for my children is to seek God's help and plead for His grace to accomplish what I am powerless to do in the heart of my child.

Saving faith for any child "is the gift of God, not a result of works, so that no one [no parent, no pastor, no grandparent, no Sunday school teacher] may boast" (Ephesians 2:8-9).

That's why being seriously committed to the discipleship of the next generation means being seriously committed to praying regularly, earnestly, and biblically for the faith of the next generation. God's power in the gospel of Jesus Christ, His unstoppable purposes for our children, and our inescapable responsibility to raise them in the faith all come together in prayer.

The night before Jesus was crucified, He told Peter, "Satan demanded to have you, that he might sift you like wheat, but I have prayed for you that your faith may not fail" (Luke 22:31-32). Isn't that amazing? Jesus, the Son of God, who sustains the universe by the word of His power, felt compelled to pray that Peter's faith would not fail after He had declared with absolute authority that this same man was the rock on which "I will build my church, and the gates of hell shall not prevail against it" (Matthew 16:18).

PRAYER AT HOME FOR THE NEXT GENERATIONS

The commitment to pray for the next generations, or for anything else, is best served by establishing a regular pattern or habit of prayer—private prayer, parental prayer, and family prayer. Home life provides many opportunities and ways to pray for children. In our home, I had the privilege of praying over our girls almost every night before they went to sleep.

As I was praying on one of those nights in the spring of 1991, an overwhelming sense of inadequacy came over me as I considered what I desired most for Amy and Kristi, alongside my profound limitations as a dad. I concluded that prayer with the benediction from Numbers 6:24-26, "The LORD bless you and keep you, the Lord make his face shine on you..."

From that evening forward, almost without exception, my final fatherly privilege of the day was to place my right hand on each daughter's head and pronounce a biblical benediction (blessing) over them. In each of those moments, my daughters witnessed their daddy express his dependence on God for the fulfillment of his heart's desire and vision for their lives.

Sally has probably prayed for the faith of our children and grandchildren more than almost anything else. Several years ago, she wrote *Praying for the Next Generation*[27], a guide to praying Scripture, which is her favorite way to pray for the next generation. We should never minimize the eternal impact of a mother's faithful prayers for the faith of her children.

For decades, I have been inspired by the example of George McClusky, who lived more than 150 years ago. He, like me, was the father of two daughters. He also was a man who understood that he

---

27 *Praying for the Next Generation* is available at Truth78.org.

could not provide what he desired most for his daughters. At some point after Bessie and Allie were born, George resolved to devote himself to praying daily from 11 a.m. to noon, not only for the spiritual welfare of his daughters but also for their children and their children's children. Only God knows all the fruit that came from those prayers, but there is substantial evidence that God's ear was inclined to hear the faithful prayers of George McClusky.

Bessie and Allie grew up, came to trust Jesus, and followed Him as Lord. The men they married both became pastors, and soon George was praying for his four granddaughters and one grandson. The four granddaughters all married pastors, and the grandson became a pastor. The first two of George's great grandchildren were both boys. One was H.B. London, who spent 30 years as a local pastor serving congregations in Oregon and California, and then 20 more years serving clergy families through his "Pastor to Pastor" ministry, before retiring and serving for another seven years as a local pastor until his death in 2018.

London's older cousin, George's first great grandchild, did not become a pastor. Instead he pursued a career in psychology, began writing books for Christian parents, founded a family ministry, and hosted a daily radio program that was eventually broadcast in more than a dozen languages on more than 7,000 stations worldwide. The program was heard daily by more than 220 million people in 164 countries, and he became the man who during the '80s and '90s was undoubtedly the most influential and significant leader of the pro-family movement that swept across America.

The Kingdom influence of that man—James Dobson—and his cousin, H.B. London, not to mention the influence of their forefathers and their descendants, is owing to God's inclination to hear the prayers of a faithful dad from five generations ago.[28]

PRAYER AT CHURCH FOR THE NEXT GENERATION

Next generation ministry in the local church should be shaped and influenced by the conviction that the "success" of that ministry depends more on "the strength that God supplies" (1 Peter 4:11) than our own efforts. How can we pray to that end?

---

[28] To read more about George McCluskey, see: James Dobson, *Your Legacy: The Greatest Gift* (New York: Faith Books, 2014), 1-6.

George Barna noticed in his research that the most effective churches in the spiritual development of their children had a significant emphasis on prayer. In his judgment, "the prayer investment of these churches may have been the single most important venture of their ministries."[29] He found that the most productive children's ministries focus their prayer in five areas: teachers praying for their students, teachers praying with other teachers, volunteer intercessors praying for teachers and students, corporate prayer for the children's ministry, and parent-led prayer for the ministry.

Teachers Praying for Their Students

Barna also noted that the most effective churches encouraged their teachers, staff, and church leaders to pray regularly for each student. Prayer goes hand in hand with faithful instruction from the Scriptures. Charles Spurgeon stressed this need to teachers:

> The Holy Scriptures must be made the means of your salvation through faith. Know the Bible, read the Bible, search the Bible, and yet that alone will not save you. What did our Lord Himself say? "You search the Scriptures, for in them you think you have eternal life; and they are they which testify of Me; and you will not come unto Me that you might have life." If you come not to Jesus, you will miss eternal life. Searching the Scriptures is able to make you wise unto salvation "through faith which is in Christ Jesus," but not without that faith. Pray, you Sunday school teachers, that you may see this faith worked in the children whom you teach. What a blessed groundwork for faith your teaching of the Holy Scriptures will be, but never mistake it for the building itself, which is of faith alone.[30]

It was always a delight for me to see teams gather together before a class or event, earnestly praying that the words of their mouths and

---

[29] George Barna, *Transforming Children into Spiritual Champions: Why Children Should Be Your Church's #1 Priority* (Ventura, Calif: Regal Books, 2003), 102.

[30] Charles Spurgeon, "The Sunday School and the Scriptures, No.1866," a sermon delivered at Metropolitan Tabernacle, Newington, England, October 18, 1885. Available at: www.spurgeongems.org

the work of their hands would bear everlasting fruit in every child. Nursery volunteers in both churches where I served understood that part of their responsibility was to make sure that every individual child was prayed for at least once during the nursery session. These prayers were guided by prayer phrases and vision statements on the walls. When the parents of these little ones were reunited with their children, their reports included that the children had been prayed for.

Team members might pray for the children as they gather ahead of time to pray that:

- the Holy Spirit be present, bringing a spirit of peace and order to our classroom.
- God would be at work causing the children to have attentive ears, minds, and hearts.
- all of our attitudes, words, and actions would serve to glorify God, edify the children, and point them to the incomparable treasure of Jesus.
- God would protect us and the children from unhelpful distractions and the darts of the enemy.
- God's Word would be clearly proclaimed by the teachers and understood by the children.
- visitors would feel loved and welcomed.
- children with special needs would be loved, served, and included.
- the children would extend grace, patience, and love to one another.
- gospel truths would be embraced with genuine faith.
- our worship time would be filled with expressions of true love and praise.
- small group leaders would be given wisdom and discernment as they seek to lead the children to respond to the truths presented.
- we would respond in wise and God-honoring ways to rebellious hearts, inattentiveness, inappropriate silliness, etc.

- parents would feel assisted and helped, and would be moved and equipped to actively disciple their children in the home.
- every child in our classroom would, by God's sovereign grace, grow and mature into a man or woman wholly devoted to Jesus Christ.[31]

Volunteer Intercessors Praying for Teachers and Students
Barna also spoke of the importance of faithful intercessors who volunteer to pray for teachers and students.[32]

For years, one of the youth ministries in our church recruited an adult prayer partner for each child in the program. The partner would commit to praying for the young person throughout the year, often resulting in a relational bond and regular prayer that lasted for many years.[33]

Corporate Prayer for the Children's Ministry
Additionally, Barna noted the importance of frequent congregational prayer for the church.[34]

In 2018, I wrote a small book entitled, *Big, Bold, Biblical Prayers for the Next Generation*,[35] a tool intended to help promote serious prayer for the discipleship of the next generation. I offered the book to anyone in the church who would be willing to read the first 30 pages and join me in weekly praying big, bold, biblical prayers.

Pastoral prayer for the next generation during the worship service also has an important place in congregational life. I have had a few opportunities to preach in the churches where I have served and many

[31] Jill Nelson, "Starting with Prayer." September 3, 2014. https://www.truth78.org/blog/post/starting-with-prayer/

[32] Barna, 103.

[33] Another strategy to consider is a "Pray for Me Campaign," http://www.prayformecampaign.com, developed by Tony Souder, founder and the CEO of One Hundred Years, a ministry dedicated to helping churches flourish in bringing the greatness of God to the next generation.

[34] Barna, 103.

[35] *Big, Bold, Biblical Prayers for the Next Generation* is available at Truth78.org.

opportunities to lead congregational prayer. At least four times a year, I was able to pray at the conclusion of our child dedication services. I discovered that as I pleaded with God on behalf of the congregation for the sake of our children with God-centered, Bible-saturated prayers, the people affirmed and embraced those desires for their own children.[36] Over the years, this has proven an effective way for not only leading the congregation in prayer for the next generation, but also instilling in the congregation a corporate vision and hope for the next generations.

Parent-Led Prayer for the Ministry

The final prayer focus that Barna identified "emanates from the parents." He wrote that some churches organize prayer times and prayer letters for parents, while others appoint elders and other prayer partners to pray specifically for parent-child requests.[37]

The bottom line is that prayer matters! It matters to us. It matters to our children. It matters because God is pleased to accomplish His unstoppable purposes through the prayers of His people. Let's boldly and biblically seek first those big and unstoppable purposes for our children, believing that all the other little concerns we have will be added to our children, for God's glory and their everlasting joy.

SUMMARY

This generation of parents, pastors, and teachers cannot escape their responsibility for nurturing the faith of the next generation, and there is no way to escape the reality that the children of the next generation will only be saved by the grace of God through faith in Jesus Christ. Saving faith for any child "is the gift of God, not a result of works, so that no one [no parent, no pastor, no grandparent, no Sunday school teacher] may boast" (Ephesians 2:8-9). God's unstoppable purposes for our children and our inescapable responsibility to raise them in the faith come together in prayer.

---

[36] Samples of these prayers are available in the back of *Big, Bold, Biblical Prayers for the Next Generation*, available at Truth78.org.
[37] Barna, 104.

Looking Ahead: *To what ultimate end do we disciple the next generations?*

COMMITMENT

7

Inspire Worship
of God, for the
Glory of God

IN BUILDINGS, THE TOPMOST or finishing stone is called
a capstone. In an arch, the capstone is the wedge-shaped stone at
the top—the final piece placed during construction that locks all
the stones into position, allowing the arch or vault to bear weight. In
seminary, I learned that there's a capstone in education, too. There, a
capstone is the culmination of academic and intellectual experience.

At the end of my time in seminary, I was expected to complete a
Statement of Faith as the capstone of all I had learned. Drawing upon
the previous years of study, I was required to capture my entire theology in a single document. Within that statement I needed to boil it
down even further to my "Integrating Motif"—a single sentence or
phrase describing the thread woven through the written revelation
of God that unified Scripture, as well as my theological convictions.

After several weeks of study, reflection, and writing, the motif I
proposed was "God and Man in Relationship." I went on to explain

that the perfect relationship between God and man was established in creation. Sin came into the world and the relationship was broken. Christ came into the world to restore the relationship and open the door for us, that by faith in Him we may enjoy a perfect relationship with the triune God forever and ever.

A NEW CAPSTONE

Fourteen years passed before I returned to that statement as preparation for my ordination. At that point, many of the great doctrines of the faith and the convictions I expressed in the 1979 document remained unchanged in my mind and heart. Enough had changed, however, that I had to do a complete rewrite of my capstone statement of faith.

One of the most dramatic changes was my integrating motif. Twelve years under the faithful preaching ministry of John Piper had transformed my understanding of God, His Word, and His ultimate purpose. In my mind, there was (and still is) only one motif that works. Just four words bring it all together for me—the glory of God.

By 1993, my eyes had been opened by John's preaching of God's Word to see that everything God has done, all that He is doing, and all that He ever will do is for His glory and His glory alone. Scripture is clear:

- God created everything to declare His glory (Psalm 19:1).

- When man sinned, we fell "short of the glory of God" (Romans 3:23).

All of God's acts past, present, and future are for the glory of His name:

- He has compassion on His people so that "Nations will fear the name of the LORD, and all the kings of the earth will fear your glory" (Psalm 102:15).

- He restrained His hand from Pharaoh in order to proclaim His name "in all the earth" (Exodus 9:16).

He acts for His glory:

- "For my own sake, for my own sake, I will do it, for how should my name be profaned? My glory I will not give to another" (Isaiah 48:11).

- God delayed His wrath for the sake of His name (Isaiah 48:9).

- God saves us for the sake of His name (Psalm 106:8).

- Jesus came for the glory of God (John 17:5).

- Jesus healed for the glory of God (John 11:4).

- Jesus prayed for the glory of God (John 17:24).

The Apostle Paul instructed us to do everything for the glory of God (1 Corinthians 10:31):

And in the end, "the earth will be filled with the knowledge of the glory of the LORD" (Habakkuk 2:14), and "every tongue [will] confess that Jesus Christ is Lord," (Philippians 2:11) "from the rising of the sun to its setting my name will be great among the nations... says the LORD of hosts" (Malachi 1:11).

ROOTED ZEAL

Zeal for the discipleship of the next generation is rooted in God's zeal for His glory.

The ultimate reason for devoting ourselves to the discipleship of the next generation is for the glory of God. That's why we and our children were created and why we exist: "bring my sons from afar and my daughters from the end of the earth, everyone who is called by my name, *whom I created for my glory,* whom I formed and made" (Isaiah 43:6-7).

If our zeal is conformed to God's zeal, and if our efforts are aligned with God's purpose, then the aim of our discipleship will be the glory of God so that His greatness and His worth will be known throughout the earth and throughout the generations.

King David shows us how this works:

> Great is the LORD, and greatly to be praised, and his greatness is unsearchable. One generation shall commend your works to another, and shall declare your mighty acts...They shall speak of the might of your awesome deeds, and I will declare your greatness. They shall pour forth the fame of your abundant goodness and shall sing aloud of your righteousness...All your works shall give thanks to you, O LORD, and all your saints shall bless you! They shall speak of the glory of your kingdom and tell of your power, to make known to the children of man your mighty deeds, and the glorious splendor of your kingdom (Psalm 145:3-4, 6-7, 10-12).

GOD'S PASSION TO MAKE HIS NAME KNOWN

As God was setting apart His people for Himself, He revealed His passion to make a name for Himself and to make it known to all peoples and to all generations. Notice the specific instructions God gave for one generation to make His name known to future generations. He told His people through Moses to devote to the LORD the first offspring of every womb so that "when in time to come your son asks you, 'What does this mean?' you shall say to him, 'By a strong hand the LORD brought us out of Egypt, from the house of slavery" (Exodus 13:14).

Moses told the people in Exodus 12:17 to take all the leavened bread out of their houses for seven days, "for on this very day I brought your hosts out of the land of Egypt. Therefore you shall observe this day, throughout your generations, as a statute forever."

In establishing the Sabbath, God said it was "a sign between me and you throughout your generations, that you may know that I, the LORD, sanctify you" (Exodus 31:13).

God established the Feast of Booths so "that your generations may know that I made the people of Israel dwell in booths when I brought them out of the land of Egypt: I am the LORD your God" (Leviticus 23:43).

God directed the Israelites to pile 12 stones on the west side of the Jordan, so that:

> "When your children ask their fathers in times to come, 'What do these stones mean?' then you shall let your children know, 'Israel passed over this Jordan on dry ground.' For the LORD your God dried up the waters of the Jordan for you until you passed over, as the Lord your God did to the Red Sea, which he dried up for us until we passed over, so that all the peoples of the earth may know that the hand of the Lord is mighty, that you may fear the Lord your God forever (Joshua 4:21-24).

NOT HIDING GOD'S GLORY

Seeing God's zeal for His glory, and His passion to make His glory known from one generation to the next, is what ignites zeal for the discipleship of the next generation. It is the reason why the fathers in Psalm 78 were commanded to teach the *"glorious* deeds of the LORD" to their children (verse 4). It is also why there is an implied warning not to hide that glory from the coming generations:

> We will not hide them from their children, but tell to the coming generation the glorious deeds of the LORD, and his might, and the wonders that he has done.

Week after week, as my eyes were being opened through John Piper's preaching of God's passion for His glory, and for making it known to the coming generations, my eyes were also being opened to see that we were in fact unwittingly hiding the glory of God from our children, and thus robbing Him of the glory that He deserved.

We were missing two obvious implications of Psalm 78:4. First, the deeds we are to tell are the LORD's deeds, and yet we were telling the stories in a way that made it look like the deeds belonged to someone else: "Esther saved her people," "Joshua defeated Jericho," "Peter healed the lame man," "Joseph interpreted the Pharaoh's dream," etc.

The second obvious implication was that if these deeds of the LORD are glorious, then the glory of the LORD is what should be magnified when telling the stories. And if the glory of the LORD is magnified, then the response of those who hear should be worship.

As the glory of God was magnified every week in worship through what John Piper calls "expository exultation,"[38] the gap was widening between my experience in corporate worship and the experience of our children and youth in Sunday school. While we were hearing of a glorious God fulfilling His promises by raising up Moses to lead His people, our children were being exhorted to be good helpers like Miriam, who helped her mother by watching her baby brother Moses in the Nile.

While our hearts soared in worshiping the "God who made the world and everything in it," and who is not "served by human hands, as though he needed anything, since he himself gives to all mankind life and breath and everything" (Acts 17:24-25), our children were learning that Jesus called His disciples because He needed helpers, and they could be His helpers, too.

While we were worshiping Jesus as the all-satisfying multiplier of fish and bread who satisfies the need and hunger of every heart, our children, hearing that 5,000 people were fed because one little boy shared his fish and bread, were discovering the importance of sharing.

There are several ways we can unwittingly hide the glory of God from our children. We can shift the attention and the glory away from God onto one or more of the biblical characters involved. We can exchange the central truth of the story for an unrelated, often moralistic idea. And we can teach what is true but put the emphasis in the wrong place. Take, for example, these three true statements:

- God loves me.
- God cares for me.
- God hears me when I pray.

All three are absolutely true, but if we make them more about me and less about God, we convey what is false and diminish God's glory.

---

[38] John Piper, *Expository Exultation: Christian Preaching as Worship* (Wheaton, Ill.: Crossway Books, 2018). Available at https://www.desiringgod.org/books/expository-exultation

Out of a sincere desire to help children feel good about themselves and feel valued by God, we might say "God loves you, cares for you, and hears you when you pray because you are so special." They may walk away feeling special, but they will also walk away with a false view of themselves and of God.

Let's consider another way to communicate the truth of these three statements:

- God is so loving and gracious that He loves undeserving sinners like you and me.
- God knows everything, and therefore He knows exactly what we need. God can do anything, and therefore He is able to give us whatever we need. God is faithful to His children, and therefore He takes care of them and will provide all that they need.
- God is constantly watching and acting in the world so nothing escapes His notice. Because God is attentive to His children, He hears them when they pray.

Hearing this, children will still feel the encouragement of God's love, knowledge, and attention, but more importantly, they will have reason to marvel at God's glory and to approach Him humbly with an accurate view of the Almighty God they are called to worship.

In one popular Bible story series, the story of Shadrach, Meshach, and Abednego concludes with "remember kids, God made you special and He loves you very much."

The well-intended writer of this story shifted the children's attention away from God and onto themselves. God did not save Shadrach, Meshach, and Abednego because they were special. God saved Shadrach, Meshach, and Abednego to demonstrate that the almighty sovereign God of the universe thwarts the evil plans of man. This God is greater than the image of gold these godly young men refused to bow down to. This God is Lord of all, and there will be no other gods before Him. These three men were special because they belonged to God, and He is always faithful to His children. He is a great God—a God "merciful and gracious, slow to anger and abounding in steadfast love and faithfulness" (Psalm 86:15).

DECLARING GOD'S GLORIOUS DEEDS LEADS TO WORSHIP

When we emphasize God's glory by declaring His glorious deeds, we are providing the God-ordained fuel for worship. Nothing in me wants to sing when you tell me how special Shadrach, Meshach, and Abednego were. But when you show me a God who rules over the forces of nature and defeats the forces of wickedness to accomplish His unstoppable purposes for His glory and the joy of His people, "then sings my soul" to the praise of God's glory and grace.

Growing up, my favorite Sunday school song (for obvious reasons) was "Only a Boy Named David." The lyrics to this song capture the storyline, but exclude the true hero. It begins...

> Only a boy named David, Only a little sling
> Only a boy named David, but he could pray and sing
> Only a boy named David, only a rippling brook
> Only a boy named David, and five little stones he took...[39]

The song continues with the boy's sling and stone going "round and round" before the stone hits its mark and causes the giant to come "tumbling down." A child may love this song and sing it with gusto, like I once did, but little did those who cared about my faith realize how that harmless song exalted "the boy named David" and reinforced my blindness to the glory of David's God.

I wonder what the response of my heart would have been if I had heard the story told this way:

> The whole army of Israel was afraid of Goliath.
> But God did not need a big army to defeat Goliath.
> God can do anything.
> And to show Israel that He can do anything,
> God used a boy with a sling and a stone to kill a giant.
> God sent David to face the giant.

---

[39] Arthur Arnott, "Only a Boy Named David" (Brentwood, Tenn: Lillenas Publishing Company, 1931).

David swung his sling around and around,
and God gave David perfect aim,
and God sent that stone right into Goliath's head.
The stone of God killed the giant Goliath.
Nothing is too hard for God!
God always defeats His enemies!

It is difficult to remember enough about my seven-year-old mind and heart to say for sure how I would have responded. I have, however, witnessed for nearly three decades how the proclamation of God's glorious deeds in a God-glorifying way inspires children to worship God for His glory and their joy in Him.

In a powerful message from Psalm 145:4, "One Generation Shall Praise Your Works to Another," John Piper states:

Praise is exultation in God. The education of the next generation must not only aim at education, it must involve exultation...Teachers and parents who do not exult over God in their teaching will not bring about exultation in God. Dry, unemotional, indifferent teaching about God—whether at home or at church—is a half-truth, at best. It says one thing about God and portrays another thing. It is inconsistent. It says that God is great, but teaches as if God is not great.[40]

The hope and vision of this seventh commitment is that our children will be God glorifiers, who give God their greatest love, honor, devotion, trust, obedience, praise, and worship. This is the only means to their all-satisfying and everlasting joy.

SUMMARY

If our zeal is conformed to God's zeal, and if our efforts are aligned with God's purpose, then the aim of our discipleship will be the glory

---

[40] John Piper, "One Generation Shall Praise Your Works to Another: Education for Exultation in the Next Generation," sermon delivered at Bethlehem Baptist Church, Minneapolis, Minn., March 19, 2000. The manuscript for this message has been included in Appendix 4.

of God so that His greatness and His worth will be known throughout the earth and throughout the generations. When we rightly emphasize God's glory when declaring His glorious deeds, the natural response of the heart is worship. The proclamation of God's *glorious deeds* in a God-glorifying way inspires children to worship God for His glory and their joy in Him.

Looking Ahead: *What if we lose zeal for these commitments of discipleship?*

Do Not Lose Heart

"Therefore, having this ministry by the mercy of God,
we do not lose heart" (2 Corinthians 4:1).

AS WE COME TO THE CLOSING chapter of a book intended to inspire zeal for the discipleship of the next generation, I am personally aware of how quickly such zeal can evaporate. For me, one of the fiercest temptations in ministry has been the temptation to lose heart.

Numerous circumstances and experiences can tempt us to lose heart in the discipleship of the next generation. We may lose zeal:

- when ministry in the church or ministry as parents is not what we expect it to be.
- when progress is slow, hindered, or absent.
- when the obstacles are overwhelming or seem impossible to overcome.
- when the fruit of our labors seem insignificant or worthless.
- when there are too many problems, too many hassles, too many difficulties, and too many demands on our time.
- when poor decisions are made that affect and undermine what we are trying to do.
- when there is too much criticism, too little cooperation, too much resistance, too little

appreciation, too many complaints, too few
encouragements, too much work, and too little support.
* when motives and actions are suspect and words are
misunderstood.
* when we feel powerless to make the changes that
need to be made.

The list can go on, and the temptations to lose heart abound!

If anyone had reason to lose heart it was the Apostle Paul, who faced hostility, opposition, a myriad of problems, and concerns of various kinds in churches he planted, not to mention threats against his life and intense physical suffering. He even experienced the ultimate discouragement of seeing the gospel "veiled to those that are perishing" by "the god of this world [who] has blinded the minds of unbelievers" in the culture (2 Corinthians 4:3, 4). Through it all, Paul resolved not to lose heart because, for him, losing heart meant losing the courage and the will to keep going. It meant giving up.

In boxing, a fighter can indicate surrender by throwing his towel into the center of the ring. To throw in the towel is to give up, signaling the end of the fight. Losing heart is like throwing in the towel. It is quitting the fight before the final bell, or stopping running in a race before you cross the finish line. It is abandoning the project before the assignment is completed. Once we lose heart, all zeal is gone.

It may be easy for us to agree that we shouldn't lose heart, but what is even more significant is recognizing the basis for our perseverance. What kept Paul pursuing ministry with zeal was knowing that his ministry was given to him "by the mercy of God." He knew it was an undeserved gift to be a servant of God entrusted with the gospel and the privilege of proclaiming it to others. This same mercy has been lavished on all believers, making us God's ambassadors who now have the ministry of proclaiming this glorious message of reconciliation through Jesus Christ and reflecting the "light of the knowledge of the glory of God" to others (verse 6). We can say with Paul, "Therefore, having this ministry by the mercy of God, we do not lose heart." We must not throw in the towel.

God forbid that any of us would lose heart for the ministry of the gospel that we have received by the mercy of God. The very thought should make us tremble. We cannot lose heart in reflecting the knowledge of the glory of God. We must not lose heart in displaying the surpassing power of Christ—to the world—or to those who are being transformed from one degree of glory to another. To throw in the towel on the gospel is to believe in vain. Paul admonished:

> Now I would remind you, brothers, of the gospel I preached to you, which you received, in which you stand, and by which you are being saved, if you hold fast to the word I preached to you—unless you believed in vain (1 Corinthians 15:1-2).

Belief is characterized by holding fast with zeal.

Paul's assignment was clearly to be "a preacher and an apostle...a teacher of the Gentiles in faith and truth" (1 Timothy 2:7). In this book, I have attempted to make the case that we, as parents, teachers, and church leaders also have a calling given by God, to pursue the discipleship of the next generation in our various roles. The seven commitments provide a vision and framework for this ministry and responsibility we have been given, by the mercy of God. So, how do we keep from joining the ranks of those who have lost their heart and thus their zeal for the discipleship of the next generation?

By reinforcing a God-centered vision for our ministry (Commitment 1), we recognize that zeal for the discipleship of the next generation is not rooted in who we are but who God is. Numerous times in 2 Corinthians, Paul demonstrates that this is how he viewed himself and the ministry that he had received by the mercy of God. Below are some other truths from this letter that God has used to sustain zeal and keep me from losing heart. May they strengthen you, too:

▾ **This is not just a job. I am more than a hireling. I am commissioned by God to minister in the sight of God.**

> For we are not, like so many, peddlers of God's word, but as men of sincerity, as commissioned by God, in the sight of God we speak in Christ (2:17).

▾ **It is not about my competency; it is about God's sufficiency to make me competent.**

...our sufficiency is from God who has made us sufficient to be ministers of a new covenant... (3:5-6).

▾ **I am just a courier who delivers the truth. Christ lifts the veil, not me. It is His glory that they behold, not mine. The "Spirit of Life" writes on the tablet of their hearts, not me.**

And you show that you are a letter from Christ delivered by us, written not with ink but with the Spirit of the living God, not on tablets of stone but on tablets of human hearts (3:3).

▾ **I am only a mirror, reflecting the light of Him who declares:**

"Let light shine out of darkness," [He] has shone in our hearts to give the light of the knowledge of the glory of God in the face of Jesus Christ (4:6).

▾ **I am a mere "jar of clay" designed by God, who chose to place His treasure in a weak, fragile, needy person.**

"...to show that the surpassing power belongs to God and not to us" (4:7).

The comparison to jars of clay reminds us that any weaknesses, limitations, and inabilities we bring are part of God's ultimate purpose to glorify Himself in our efforts and to show His power at work in our zeal.

[Because we are jars of clay, we] are afflicted in every way...[but because of the surpassing power of God, we are]...not crushed (4:8).

[Because we are jars of clay, we are] perplexed...[but because of the surpassing power of God, we are]...not driven to despair (4:8).

[Because we are jars of clay, we are] persecuted....[but because of the surpassing power of God, we are] not forsaken (4:9).

[Because we are jars of clay, we are] struck down [but because of the surpassing power of God, we are] not destroyed (4:9).

[Because we are jars of clay, we are] always carrying in the body the death of Jesus...[but because of the surpassing power of God]...the life of Jesus may also be manifested in our bodies (4:10).

Paul's jar of clay was lacerated at least 195 times with a whip. Three times it was beaten with rods. Once it was stoned. Three times it was shipwrecked. It was adrift at sea for a night and a day. It was in danger from rivers, danger from robbers, danger from Jews, danger from Gentiles, danger in the city, danger in the wilderness, danger at sea, danger from false brothers. It endured toil and hardship, through many a sleepless night, in hunger and thirst, often without food, in cold and exposure. Beyond all of this he had the daily pressure of anxiety for all the churches (11:25-28). Yet, his response is striking:

If I must boast, I will boast in the things that show my weakness (11:30).

There was also a "thorn" given to Paul, which he said was "a messenger of Satan" to harass his jar of clay. Three times Paul "pleaded with the Lord" to remove it, but the Lord instead reminded Paul of the source of his endurance and his protection from losing heart:

But he said to me, "My grace is sufficient for you, for my power is made perfect in weakness" (12:9).

Therefore, Paul gladly boasted in the weaknesses of his jar of clay,

...so that the power of Christ may rest upon me. For the sake of Christ, then, I am content with weaknesses, insults, hardships, persecutions, and calamities. For when I am weak, then I am strong (12:9-10).

And so we can say, "Therefore, having this ministry by the mercy of God, we do not lose heart."

As Jesus and His disciples were making their way to Jerusalem, He knew His death was imminent. One of the ways He prepared them for His departure was by telling them a story, which Luke said was to remind them that "they ought always to pray and not lose heart" (Luke 18:1). It was the familiar story of the persistent widow who kept appealing to the unrighteous judge. We might say that she was a woman who was "zealous" for her cause.

After telling the story, Jesus made His point:

> "Hear what the unrighteous judge says. And will not God give justice to his elect, who cry to him day and night? Will he delay long over them? I tell you, he will give justice to them speedily" (18:6-9a).

His point is clear. This woman prevailed in her appeal to a wicked, unjust, god-forsaking judge. How much more shall we prevail in our appeal to our righteous Father in heaven?

This woman was a stranger to the judge; we are the beloved children of God. She was all by herself; we are among many who approach the throne together, united in our appeal.

She had none but herself to plead her cause, but we have an Advocate appealing to His Father on our behalf.

She was ignored and avoided while we are welcomed into the presence of the Lord. She had limited access; yet we can come any moment, day or night.

She was given no encouragement to ask for help and had little hope of getting it. We are told to come and ask with confidence that we shall receive. Her persistence provoked the judge, while our persistence pleases the Lord.

If this woman did not lack zeal in taking her cause to an unrighteous judge, how much more zealous should we be in taking our cause to our Righteous Father?

"Therefore, having this ministry [the discipleship of the next generation], by the mercy of God, we do not lose heart."

Any difficulty we experience, any affliction we suffer, and any opposition we face is worth it. "For this light momentary affliction is preparing for us [and, we trust, for our children] an eternal weight of glory beyond all comparison" (2 Corinthians 4:17). On the days when it seems like we are "being given over to death for Jesus' sake," we can rejoice that "the life of Jesus [that is] manifested in our mortal flesh" is producing fruit in us and in the next generation that has value far beyond what we are able to see (verses 10-11).

May this reality strengthen our hearts and enable us to persevere in this ministry that we have by the mercy of God. May God forbid that we—as parents, grandparents, teachers, pastors, and all who are investing in the faith of the next generations—would lose heart. With our hope secure in all that God is and all that He has promised to be, may we be fervent in spirit and in the strength that God provides, as we resolve to:

- Embrace a biblical vision for the faith of the next generation.
- Foster a robust partnership between church and home.
- Teach the breadth and depth of the whole counsel of God.
- Proclaim the glorious gospel of Jesus Christ.
- Disciple the mind, heart, and will.
- Pray with dependence on God's sovereign grace.
- Inspire worship of God, for the glory of God.

Do all this with zeal! Do it all for the unshakable hope and eternal joy of the next generations.

And "Now to him who is able to do far more abundantly than all that we ask or think, according to the power at work within us, to him be the glory in the church and in Christ Jesus *throughout all generations,* forever and ever" (Ephesians 3:20-21).

▼ ▼ ▼

Will you be zealous for
the discipleship of the
next generations?

Will you make the
seven commitments
your own?

Will you apply them in
your discipleship as a parent,
a grandparent, a teacher,
a pastor, or whatever role
God has given you with
the next generation?

*GO TO **TRUTH78.ORG/ZEALOUS** TO FIND
SUPPORT AND ENCOURAGEMENT FOR GROWING
IN ZEAL AND APPLYING THESE COMMITMENTS
FOR THE JOY OF THE NEXT GENERATIONS.*

Acknowledgements

MY NAME SHOULD not be the only one on the front of this book. Apart from the grace of God, who loves to magnify His strength in our weakness and abundantly exceed what we ask or think, this book would not exist.

This grace of God was manifest in the person of my wife. Sally's zeal for the discipleship of the next generation has had a contagious effect on me. Even more, she has influenced the vision and convictions that have shaped these seven commitments and have defined our philosophy of parenting and ministry to children and youth over the years. Many of the concepts and ideas in this book have their roots in content that Sally developed for various workshops, classes, and conference messages that we have presented over the past three decades. She is not only a serious student of the Bible, but she is also a gifted teacher who knows how to communicate with children. This has made her an invaluable and indispensable partner with me in parenting and in ministry to parents, children, and youth.

In one sense John Piper had nothing to do with this book, and in another sense he had everything to do with it. It would be difficult to overstate how God has used the influence of John's radically God-centered preaching and teaching ministry to bring this book and the ministry of Truth78 into being. His Bible-saturated passion for God and for the truth about Him has ignited and sustained in Sally and me and in our colleagues at Truth78 a zeal for the discipleship of the next generation.

Our focus on the word "zealous" and the seven commitments was born on a prayer and planning retreat followed by several weeks of discussion, wordsmithing, and prioritizing in the fall of 2019. I thank God for Brian Eaton, Steve Watters, Dan Dumas, Jill Nelson, Gary Brewer, and Sally Michael, who gave themselves to the task of producing a concise yet comprehensive expression of the convictions and mission that define Truth78. The substance of this book is the fruit of those discussions and the collective insights and wisdom of these faithful co-laborers in ministry.

Upholding this effort has been a devoted and remarkably gifted Truth78 staff, board of directors, and ministry partners who are pursuing this vision with us. They have faithfully prayed and invested time and resources to support this effort. Together, our earnest desire is to serve the Church and to promote a biblical vision for the discipleship and the everlasting joy of the next generation. I will be forever grateful to God for these precious partners in ministry.

To God be the glory in the Church and in Christ Jesus to all generations!

Appendix 1

Resources Supporting Commitments

The following resources and training materials related to each commitment are available from, or recommended by, Truth78. Training is available at **Truth78.org/training** and resources are available at **Truth78.org/products**.

Embrace a biblical vision for the faith of the next generation.

- Foundations for ministry (truth78.org/foundations-for-ministry)
- *Indestructible Joy for the Next Generations*

Foster a robust partnership between church and home.

- Partnering with Your Church (truth78.org/partnering-with-your-church)
- Partnering with Parents (truth78.org/partnering-with-parents)
- *Children in the Worship Service*

Teach the breadth and depth of the whole counsel of God.

- Sunday School, Midweek Bible, Intergenerational, and Backyard Bible Club/VBS curricula (truth78.org/curriculum-introduction)
- Scope and sequence explanation (truth78.org/scope-sequence-explanation)

Proclaim the glorious gospel of Jesus Christ.

- *Helping Children to Understand the Gospel*
- *God's Gospel*
- *Established in the Faith*
- *Glorious God, Glorious Gospel*
- *The World Created, Fallen, Redeemed, Restored*

Disciple the mind, heart, and will.

- Scope and sequence explanation (truth78.org/scope-sequence-explanation)
- *Discipleship through Doctrinal Teaching and Catechism*
- *Mothers: Disciplers of the Next Generations*

Recommended resources for Christian education directors

- *Teaching to Change Lives: Seven Proven Ways to Make Your Teaching Come Alive* by Dr. Howard Hendricks
- *Creative Bible Teaching* by Lawrence O. Richards and Gary J. Bredfeldt

Recommended resources for parents

- *Gospel-Powered Parenting: How the Gospel Shapes and Transforms Parenting* by William P. Farley
- *The Disciple-Making Parent: A Comprehensive Guidebook for Raising Your Children to Love and Follow Jesus Christ* by Chap Bettis

- *Teach them Diligently: How to Use the Scriptures in Child Training* by Lou Priolo
- *Shepherding a Child's Heart* by Tedd Tripp
- *Instructing a Child's Heart* by Tedd and Margy Tripp

Pray with dependence on God's sovereign grace.

- *Big, Bold, Biblical Prayers for the Next Generation*
- *Praying for the Next Generation*
- *A Father's Guide to Blessing His Children*
- *Utter Dependency on God, Through Prayer*

Inspire worship of God, for the glory of God.

- *A Vision for God-Centered, Gospel-Focused Teaching for the Next Generations,* video by David and Sally Michael sharing the foundations of a God-centered children's ministry (truth78.org/foundations-for-ministry)

ADDITIONAL RESOURCES FOR DISCIPLING CHILDREN

- Fighter Verses (fighterverses.com)
- *The Inductive Bible Study Handbook* (truth78.org/the-inductive-bible-study-handbook-print)
- Making HIM Known books (truth78.org/products/making-him-known)
- *When I Am Afraid* (truth78.org/when-i-am-afraid)
- *More Than a Story: Old Testament*—A new kind of Bible resource for children, a book that takes them on a chronological journey through the Bible with a God-centered, gospel-focused, discipleship-oriented, theologically grounded perspective. (truth78.org/story)

Appendix 2

Vision for the Next Generations

College Park Church • Indianapolis, Indiana • 5-4-15

VISION SUMMARY

The Next Generation Passionately Following Jesus

VISION STATEMENT

To ignite a passion in the next generations at College Park Church to passionately follow Jesus with the aim to be God-centered, Christ-exalting, Spirit-dependent, Bible-saturated, doctrinally-grounded, faith-filled, mission-minded, spiritually-mature men and women of God.

GOD-CENTERED

"So, whether you eat or drink, or whatever you do, do all to the glory of God" (1 Corinthians 10:31).

Our aim is that the next generation will recognize the supremacy of God and embrace His ultimate purpose to glorify Himself in all things; and live lives that manifest that purpose by desiring Him, fearing Him, delighting in Him, obeying Him, trusting Him, admiring Him and being completely satisfied in Him more than anything else and declare His glory from generation to generation.

Our prayer is that:

- our children would read the Bible with God-centered eyes to the glory of his name.
- the attention of our children would be drawn to God.
- the next generation will worship, admire and exalt the splendor and majesty of God forever and ever.
- they would pursue a God-centered vision for their lives (Romans 11:36).
- they would fear God and delight in all his ways (Deuteronomy 10:12).
- the centrality of God will be a constant refrain in all that we do for the next generations.
- together with all of creation our children would declare the glory of God and to honor His name forever (Isaiah 43:7).

CHRIST-EXALTING

"Therefore God has highly exalted him and bestowed on him the name that is above every name, so that at the name of Jesus every knee should bow, in heaven and on earth and under the earth, and every tongue confess that Jesus Christ is Lord, to the glory of God the Father" (Philippians 2:9-11).

Our aim is that the words, thoughts, decisions, and deeds of our children will be done in the name of Christ, by His power, and according to His grace so that in everything Christ might be preeminent (Colossians 1:18) and be glorified in them and they in him as their supreme treasure (Romans 11:36; Colossians 3:17; 2 Thessalonians 1:11-12).

Our prayer is that:
- the next generations might possess a deep and abiding love for Christ (John 15:4-6).
- Jesus Christ might be their Lord, their Savior, their King and their greatest treasure.
- the next generation would taste and see the all-satisfying glory of our Lord Jesus Christ.
- Christ might be for our children the ever-present and highest aim of all their actions and thoughts and feelings.
- the feet of our children will one day stand before the throne and before the Lamb, and their ears will hear him say, "Well done, good and faithful servant. You have been faithful over a little; I will set you over much. Enter into the joy of your master" (Matthew 25:23).

SPIRIT-DEPENDENT

"And I was with you in weakness and in fear and much trembling, and my speech and my message were not in plausible words of wisdom, but in demonstration of the Spirit and of power, so that your faith might not rest in the wisdom of men but in the power of God" (1 Corinthians 2:3-5).

Our aim is that our children will learn to rely on the Holy Spirit for strength in weakness, boldness in witness, hope in adversity and power to live lives that are rooted in love, joy, peace, patience, kindness, goodness, faithfulness, gentleness, self-control (Galatians 5:22-23); and obtain the strength to comprehend with all the saints what is the breadth and length and height and depth, and to know the love of Christ that surpasses knowledge, that they may be filled with all the fullness of God (Ephesians 3:18-19).

Our prayer is that:
- our children would have unleashed energy, creativity and gifts for the sake of the Gospel and the joy of the generations to come.

- our children would be unyielding to the "spirit of the age" (1 Corinthians 2:12).
- their thoughts, conduct and character that have the aroma of Christ (2 Corinthians 2:15).
- they would have minds that dwell on things which are true, honorable, just, pure, lovely, commendable, excellent, and worthy of praise (Philippians 4:8).

BIBLE-SATURATED

"Blessed is the man who walks not in the counsel of the wicked, nor stands in the way of sinners, nor sits in the seat of scoffers; but his delight is in the law of the LORD, and on his law he meditates day and night" (Psalm 1:1-2).

Our aim is that the next generation will be joyfully immersed in the Bible through study, meditation, and memorization making them wise for salvation through faith in Christ Jesus (2 Timothy 3:15) and that the Word will shape their understanding of God, themselves, and the world in which they live and influence every area of their lives including their conversations, their prayers, their thoughts, their affections, their counsel, their decisions, their attitudes, their opinions and their priorities.

Our conviction is that:
- it is through the revelation given to us in the Bible that our children learn who God is, what He has done, His good purposes, how He saves His people from their sin, and how we are to rightly respond to Him (2 Timothy 3:16-17; John 20:31).
- we must teach children to correctly read and understand the Bible, encouraging them toward thoughtful examination and careful interpretation of Bible passages.

Our prayer is that our children would:
- possess a storehouse of Bible verses committed to memory.
- have unshakable confidence in God's unchanging Word.
- rightly handle the Word of truth (2 Timothy 2:15).
- be grounded in the Word of God.
- have speech that is seasoned with the Word of God flowing out of a storehouse of memorized scripture.
- embrace the Bible for the treasure that it is.
- "from childhood" know the Bible so they can know the God of the Bible (2 Timothy 3:15).
- be Bible-saturated people who look for answers to the questions of life in the book of life.
- be Bible-saturated people who have an ever-present counselor, comforter and interpreter.

Our vision is to:
- raise up from our nurseries another generation of Bible-saturated men and women of God who passionately follow our Lord Jesus Christ.
- partner with parents to teach the Word of God so that our children will know the Word of God and passionately follow our Lord Jesus Christ.
- acquaint our children with as much of Scripture as they can absorb rather than bore them with shallow presentations of watered-down truth.
- to see an aged man, silenced and immobilized by a stroke yet clinging with joy to a verse he has known from childhood—"Whom have I in heaven but you? And there is nothing on earth that I desire besides you. My flesh and my heart may fail, but God is the strength of my heart and my portion forever" (Psalm 73:25-26).

DOCTRINALLY-GROUNDED

"But as for you, teach what accords with sound doctrine" (Titus 2:1).

Our aim is that the next generation will be equipped for seeing, understanding and embracing the whole counsel of God, and the glory of His attributes, the splendor of His majesty, the perfection of His ways, the beauty of the Gospel according to His redemptive purposes, so that they can know Him for who He is and trust Him for all that He has promised; discern anything contrary to His Word and His will and be well-equipped for the work of the ministry.

Our conviction is that we must:
• teach children all the essential doctrines of the Christian faith (Colossians 1:28; Acts 20:26-28; Titus 2:1) and strive to impart the whole counsel of God through a Bible-story based chronological exposure to the Bible, a biblical theology of the main storyline of the Bible, a systematic theology of foundational doctrines, an exposure to the Bible as moral instruction and an ethical theology, and an explicit presentation of the Gospel of Jesus Christ; and to teach them the skills to rightly understand and interpret the Bible.
• give our children big truths that are expressed and explained through easily understood terms and illustrations.
• resist avoiding difficult doctrines, but teach them in a manner that is age appropriate and creatively engaging in the hope that the Holy Spirit will grant understanding and growth through the faithful teaching of the Word (Acts 20:26-28; 2 Timothy 2:7).
• aim for our children to be firmly established in faith and doctrine so that they might be secure in their convictions, unyielding to the "spirit of the age" and faithful to Christ.

Our belief is that:
- right theology sustains authentic doxology.
- education undergirds exultation.
- what is learned in childhood is often retained for a lifetime.

To the end that:
- our children might have truth-shaped appetites, attitudes, and actions.

FAITH-FILLED

"I have been crucified with Christ. It is no longer I who live, but Christ who lives in me. And the life I now live in the flesh I live by faith in the Son of God, who loved me and gave himself for me" (Galatians 2:20).

Our aim is that the next generation will be equipped for living by faith in the Son of God, walking in His ways, trusting Him in every circumstance, standing firm against the schemes of the devil, holding fast with confidence in His goodness, resting in his sovereignty, running with endurance the race that is set before us, persevering in the full assurance of hope, pressing on toward the goal for the prize of the upward call of God in Christ Jesus, faithful to the end.

Our prayer is that the next generation:
- be unshakably standing on the promises of God.
- possess an enduring faith that will remain steadfast when inevitable trouble comes (Psalm 125:1).
- be equipped to weather the storms of life.
- might know the testimony and the work of God, the children yet unborn, and arise and tell them to their children, so that they might set their hope in God and not forget the works of God... (Psalm 78:6-7).

SPIRITUALLY MATURE

"Him we proclaim, warning everyone and teaching everyone
with all wisdom, that we may present everyone mature in Christ"
(Colossians 1:28).

Our aim is that the next generation will walk in the wisdom
of God with simplicity, godly sincerity, self-control and sober-
mindedness possessing the discernment to distinguish good
from evil (Hebrews 5:14); and be grown up in every way into
Christ (Ephesians 4:11-16).

Our prayer is that our children:
- are able to embrace and apply a biblical
  understanding of manhood and womanhood.
- be disciplined in worship, study, prayer
  and ministry.
- be well-integrated into the life and ministry
  of the church.
- understand and effectively use their gifts.
- develop and maintain strong, life-giving, balanced
  relationships with peers, parents and other adults.
- be inspired by the example of parents, nursery
  workers, Sunday school teachers and youth leaders
  who faithfully impart the full counsel of God.
- be equipped, encouraged, inspired and supported
  for raising their children in the faith.

MISSION-MINDED

"But you will receive power when the Holy Spirit has come upon you, and you will be my witnesses in Jerusalem and in all Judea and Samaria, and to the end of the earth" (Acts 1:8).

Our aim is that the next generation will be courageous, well-equipped, gospel-telling, world-Christians who can winsomely engage the culture for the sake of Christ and who are devoted to advancing the glory of God and the spreading of his praise for the joy of the nations, the neighborhoods, and the generations to come.

Our prayer is that our children would be:
- informed and invested in proclaiming Christ to the nations.
- thoughtfully, winsomely and fruitfully engaged in the "Next Door Mission" of the church.
- living courageously in the world even under pressure to conform.
- influencing culture for the sake of Christ.
- laboring with joy and a sense of calling on their lives.
- Bible-based, prayer-soaked, mission grounded in passion for the glory of God.

To the end that the next generation might know the praiseworthy deeds of God. And arise and tell them to their children (Psalm 78:6).

Appendix 3

10 Essential Gospel Truths

1. God is the sovereign Creator of all things.

    Scripture: *Psalm 19:1, Psalm 22:28; Psalm 24:1; Isaiah 44:24*
    Implication ▾ God made you. You belong to God.
God is your ruler.

2. God created people for His glory.

    Scripture: *Psalm 29:1-2; Isaiah 43:6-7; 1 Corinthians 10:31*
    Implication ▾ God created you to know, trust, and
love Him most of all.

3. God is holy and righteous.

    Scripture: *Leviticus 19:2, 37; Deuteronomy 32:4; Romans 7:12*
    Implication ▾ God's commands are holy and righteous.
You must obey God's commands all the time.

4. Man is sinful.

    Scripture: *Romans 3:10-18, 20, 23*
    Implication ▾ You have disobeyed God's commands.
You are a sinner.

5. God is just and is right to punish sin.

Scripture: Isaiah 59:2; Romans 1:18; Romans 6:23a
Implication ▾ You deserve God's punishment of death and hell. You are helpless to save yourself.

6. God is merciful. He is kind to undeserving sinners.

Scripture: Psalm 145:8; Ephesians 2:8-9
Implication ▾ You must depend on God's mercy in order to be saved.

7. Jesus is God's holy and righteous Son.

Scripture: John 1:1; 1 Timothy 1:15
Implication ▾ Jesus came into the world to save you.

8. God put the punishment of sinners on Jesus, so that His righteousness might be put on them.

Scripture: Isaiah 53:5; Romans 5:8; 2 Corinthians 5:21; 1 Peter 2:24
Implication ▾ Jesus died on the cross to be punished in your place.

9. God offers the free gift of salvation to those who repent and believe in Jesus.

Scripture: Mark 1:15; John 3:16-17; Acts 4:12; Ephesians 2:8-9
Implication ▾ God tells you to believe in Jesus
and repent of your sins and you will be saved.

10. Those who trust in Jesus will live to please Him and will receive the promise of eternal life—enjoying God forever in heaven.

Scripture: Luke 9:23; John 11:25; 1 John 2:15; Psalm 16:11
Implication ▾ If you are trusting in Jesus for your
salvation, you must follow Him. Jesus has promised
that when you die He will bring you to heaven to live
with and enjoy God forever.

These essential truths are developed further in the booklet *Helping Children to Understand the Gospel,* which includes a fuller explanation of the essential truths and child-appropriate teaching of them. This resource also helps parents discern stages of spiritual growth and prepare the hearts of their children to hear the gospel.

Appendix 4

One Generation Shall Praise Your Works to Another

Education for Exultation in
the Next Generation[1]

JOHN PIPER, BETHLEHEM BAPTIST CHURCH

One generation shall praise Your works to another,
And shall declare Your mighty acts. Psalm 145:4

THE RESPONSIBILITY OF EACH GENERATION TO THE NEXT

It is the Biblical duty of every generation of Christians to see to it that the next generation hears about the mighty acts of God. God does not drop a new Bible from heaven on every generation. He intends that the older generation will teach the newer generation to read and think and trust and obey and rejoice. It's true that God draws near personally to every new generation of believers, but he does so through the Biblical truth that they learn from the preceding generations. The

[1] https://www.desiringgod.org/messages/
one-generation-shall-praise-your-works-to-another

Spirit comes down vertically (you might say) where the truth of God is imparted horizontally.

But there is another reason that Psalm 145:4 is so relevant to our theme this morning. Not only does it speak of the imparting of truth from one generation to another, it speaks of a certain kind of imparting. It is an imparting with exultation and for exultation. Notice the words. It does not say, "One generation shall merely teach Your works to another." It says, "One generation shall praise Your works to another." Praise is exultation in God. The education of the next generation must not only aim at education it must involve exultation.

Teachers and parents who do not exult over God in their teaching will not bring about exultation in God. Dry, unemotional, indifferent teaching about God—whether at home or at church—is a half-truth, at best. It says one thing about God and portrays another thing. It is inconsistent. It says that God is great, but teaches as if God is not great.

Psalm 145:4 shows us another way: "One generation shall praise Your works to another." Let praises carry the truth to the next generation, because the aim of truth is praise. The aim of education is exultation. So let education model exultation in the way it is done.

"INFATUATED WITH THE KINGDOM"

Now let me build a bridge from last week's message to this one. I said last week that our aim in the coming decades will be to breed children and young people here at Bethlehem who are radically surrendered to Jesus and radically committed to his cause of world evangelization. By "radically committed," we mean so deeply committed that no price is too high to pay to follow Jesus wherever he leads, no matter how distant or how dangerous.

One of you sent me a quote from Jim Elliot's journals to underscore this aim and say amen.

At age 22, Jim Elliot had a promising ministry in front of him in the United States. He probably could have been a very successful pastor or evangelist or teacher. His parents were not very excited about his call to go to the Quichuas in South America. They wrote and told him so. He answered bluntly.

"I do not wonder that you were saddened at the word of my going to South America," he replied on August 8. This is nothing else than what the Lord Jesus warned us of when He told the disciples that they must become so infatuated with the kingdom and following Him that all other allegiances must become as though they were not. And He never excluded the family tie. In fact, those loves that we regard as closest, He told us must become as hate in comparison with our desires to uphold His cause. Grieve not, then, if your sons seem to desert you, but rejoice, rather, seeing the will of God done gladly. Remember how the Psalmist described children? He said that they were as an heritage from the Lord, and that every man should be happy who had his quiver full of them. And what is a quiver full of but arrows? And what are arrows for but to shoot? So, with the strong arms of prayer, draw the bowstring back and let the arrows fly—all of them, straight at the Enemy's hosts.

Give of thy sons to bear the message glorious,
Give of thy wealth to speed them on their way,
Pour out thy soul for them in prayer victorious,
And all thou spendest Jesus will repay.[2]

That's what Education for Exultation in the Next Generation is about: to breed that kind of child and teenager and young adult. Where will they come from? That kind of 22-year-old doesn't grow on trees. Where do they come from? That is what I want to talk about today.

The answer is that they come from God. God makes hearts like that. And he is sovereign: he can make such a heart in a dysfunctional family and a failing church. But that is not his ordinary way, and it is not the way he commands. His ordinary way is to breed hearts like that in God-exalting families and in churches where "One generation shall praise Your works to another."

Notice one key word in Jim Elliot's explanation to his parents. He said, "[Jesus] told the disciples that they must become so infatuated

[2] Elisabeth Elliot, *Shadow of the Almighty: The Life and Testament of Jim Elliot* (New York: Harper & Brothers Publishers, 1958), 132. (This is a quotation from a hymn titled, "Oh, Zion Haste.")

with the kingdom and following Him that all other allegiances must become as though they were not." Why the word "infatuated"? Because Christianity is more than right thinking about the kingdom. It is also right feeling about the kingdom. It is right allegiance to the kingdom. It is not just education about following Jesus; it is exultation in following Jesus.

That's the link with Psalm 145:4: "One generation shall praise Your works to another, and declare your mighty acts." What we want from the next generation is not just heads full of right facts about the works of God; we want heads full of right facts and hearts that burn with the fire of love for the God of those facts—hearts that will sell everything to follow Jesus into the hardest places of the world.

CONVICTIONS THAT SHAPE THE WAY WE EDUCATE

So how shall we do this? How shall we do education and exultation for the next generation at Bethlehem? I'll mention three convictions or principles that will shape the way we aim to shape children and young people. I will try to show Biblical texts that support these three principles. Psalm 145:4 gives the overarching aim: "One generation shall praise Your works to another." These other texts tell us how.

1. PARENTS EDUCATE THEIR CHILDREN

Foundational to all our ministry to children and young people is that God's ordinary way of shaping children into radically committed, risk-taking, countercultural, wise, thinking, loving, mature, world Christians is through parents who teach and model a God-centered, Bible-saturated worldview to their children. Why do we start with that conviction? Because Deuteronomy 6:4-7 says,

> Hear, O Israel! The LORD is our God, the LORD is one! You shall love the LORD your God with all your heart and with all your soul and with all your might. These words, which I am commanding you today, shall be on your heart. You shall teach them diligently to your sons and shall talk of them when you sit in your house and when you walk by the way and when you lie down and when you rise up. (See also Deuteronomy 11:19.)

Centuries later, Asaph says in Psalm 78:5-7:

[The LORD] established a testimony in Jacob
And appointed a law in Israel,
Which He commanded our fathers
That they should teach them to their children,
That the generation to come might know,
Even the children yet to be born,
That they may arise and tell them to their children,
That they should put their confidence in God
And not forget the works of God,
But keep His commandments.

And in the New Testament, Ephesians 6:1-4 says: "Children, obey your parents in the Lord, for this is right. HONOR YOUR FATHER AND MOTHER (which is the first commandment with a promise), SO THAT IT MAY BE WELL WITH YOU, AND THAT YOU MAY LIVE LONG ON THE EARTH. Fathers, do not provoke your children to anger, but bring them up in the discipline and instruction of the Lord."

The Biblical pattern is for parents, especially fathers, not to relinquish their role as the primary teachers and shapers of their children's mind and heart—not even to the church. The Biblical pattern is for parents to impart to their children a God-centered, Bible-saturated vision for all of life. Education for Exultation is not primarily a vision of how to replace parents with church, but to restore parents to their God-ordained role. This is one reason why David and Sally Michael are called Pastor and Minister for Parenting and Children's Discipleship, not simply Pastor and Minister for Children.

That's principle #1: Parents educate their children.

2. THE CHURCH IS A PARTNER WITH THE PARENTS IN EDUCATING THE CHILDREN

There are lots of reasons why this is important. Practical ones include the facts that 1) some children don't have believing parents; 2) some single parent homes are so stressed and overworked that they need all the help they can get; 3) there is a whole range of competencies in moms and dads that may need supplementing in the world the way it is (if not the way it should be); 4) even the best home-teaching will benefit from reinforcement in a corporate setting; and 5) some aspects of God's character may be caught better in a larger corporate setting than at home.

On this last point consider Deuteronomy 31:10-13: Moses commanded them, saying, "At the end of every seven years, at the time of the year of remission of debts, at the Feast of Booths, when all Israel comes to appear before the LORD your God at the place which He will choose, you shall read this law in front of all Israel in their hearing. Assemble the people, the men and the women and children and the alien who is in your town, so that they may hear and learn and fear the LORD your God, and be careful to observe all the words of this law. Their children, who have not known, will hear and learn to fear the Lord your God, as long as you live on the land which you are about to cross the Jordan to possess."

Notice those words in verse 13, "Their children who have not known..." Does this mean that Moses assumes that fathers will be delinquent, and a corporate gathering every seven years will make up the difference? Probably not. Rather, it probably means that there are some things that are going to be picked up and seen and felt in this kind of gathering that would not ordinarily be picked up at home. Peter Craigie takes the meaning to be that

"The function of the ceremony would be educational...The younger generation, however, would learn for the first time the full meaning of the covenant (v.13). Although they would know about it beforehand, its significance would dawn on them fully only as they left their homes and villages and heard the public reading of the law in the presence of all Israel (cf. v.11)."[3]

One lesson to draw from this is that church education can be an important supplement and reinforcement to what parents do at home. Therefore partnership between parents and church is the image we see for Bethlehem.

There is a pointer in the New Testament that the Jewish people did not understand the passages about home teaching to rule out the

---

[3] Peter C. Craigie, *The Book of Deuteronomy* (Grand Rapids, Mich.: William B. Eerdmans Publishing Co., 1976), 371.

supplementing of education from others who have a special expertise. In Acts 22:3, Paul was making his defense before the Jews, and said, "I am a Jew, born in Tarsus of Cilicia, but brought up in this city, educated under Gamaliel, strictly according to the law of our fathers, being zealous for God just as you all are today." Notice the reference "educated under Gamaliel"—literally "at the feet of Gamaliel." This was the usual place for the younger students of a gifted rabbi to sit as they were instructed. This does not mean that the parents were delinquent. It means that when we say parents have primary responsibility to shape their children's mind and heart, we don't mean that they cannot or should not avail themselves of gifted teachers to supplement their own efforts.

3. THE CHURCH HELPS EQUIP THE PARENTS TO EDUCATE THE CHILDREN

When children grow up and become adults, they don't cease to learn and grow—at least they should not (see 2 Peter 3:18; 1 Corinthians 14:20). And as some of them move toward parenting and teaching children, they must continue to be taught and shaped biblically, and the church has a high calling to see this happen.

Moses says to the people (in Deuteronomy 4:9), "Give heed to yourself and keep your soul diligently, so that you do not forget the things which your eyes have seen and they do not depart from your heart all the days of your life; but make them known to your sons and your grandsons." First, Moses must minister to the people and they must give heed to themselves and their own souls. Then they will be able to teach their children.

So in the New Testament, Paul says in Ephesians 4:11-12, "[Christ] gave some as apostles, and some as prophets, and some as evangelists, and some as pastors and teachers, for the equipping of the saints for the work of service, to the building up of the body of Christ." Pastors and teachers equip the saints to do the work of the ministry—the ministry of parenting and the ministry of teaching Sunday School and Kids' Connection and a hundred other ways to nurture others, young and old.

Which means, in summary, that Education for Exultation—in the next Generation is three things: 1) parents educate their children; 2) the Church is a partner with the parents in educating the children; and 3) the Church helps equip the parents and others to educate the children.

And if you have eyes to see, you will know that in this last point everyone is included. The church that educates only children with Biblical truth will get shallower and shallower and shallower, until the reservoir of Biblical doctrine is so small that no one can drink there and find the words of life. And where there was perhaps once a robust Bible-teaching, Christ-exalting, mission-minded church, there is now only a Bible-neglecting, God-belittling, social Christianity.

To guard against that, and to keep the reservoir of truth and doctrine full and deep and pure enough to drink—for all ages—is the aim of Education for Exultation—in the next Generation. I hope and pray that you will be part of it.

Truth78

TRUTH78 is a vision-oriented ministry for the next generations—that they may know, honor, and treasure God, setting their hope in Christ alone, so that they will live as faithful disciples for the glory of God.

Our mission is to nurture the faith of the next generations by equipping the church and home with resources and training that instruct the mind, engage the heart, and influence the will through proclaiming the whole counsel of God.

EQUIP YOUR CHURCH AND HOME

Truth78 offers the following categories of resources and training materials for the church and home:

VISION-CASTING AND TRAINING

We offer opportunities to grow in biblical vision, encouragement, and practical applications for ministry to the next generations through a wide variety of booklets, video and audio seminars, articles, and other practical training resources that highlight and expound our vision, mission, and values, as well as our educational philosophy and methodology. Many of these resources are freely distributed through our website to help ministry leaders, volunteers, and parents implement Truth78's vision and mission in their churches and homes. By subscribing to the Truth78 e-newsletter (**Truth78.org/enewsletter**), you will receive weekly updates on new articles and resources.

CURRICULUM

We publish materials designed for formal Bible instruction. The scope and sequence of these materials reflects our commitment to teach children and youth the whole counsel of God over the course of their education. Materials include curricula for Sunday schools, midweek Bible programs, Backyard Bible Clubs or vacation Bible schools, and intergenerational studies. Most of these materials can be adapted for use in Christian schools and education in the home. Learn more at **Truth78.org/curriculum-introduction**.

PARENTING AND FAMILY DISCIPLESHIP

We have produced a variety of materials and training resources designed to help parents disciple their children, including booklets, video presentations, family devotionals, children's books, and articles. Our curricula also include parent pages to help apply what is taught in the classroom to their children's daily experience in order to nurture faith. Our *More Than a Story* resource is a discipleship tool that explores the message of the Bible with children so they will know, understand, and embrace the truths of Scripture. Learn more at **Truth78.org/family-overview**.

BIBLE MEMORY

Our Fighter Verses™ Bible memory program is designed to encourage churches, families, and individuals in the lifelong practice and love of Bible memory. The program offers an easy-to-use Bible memory system with carefully chosen verses to help fight the fight of faith. It is available in print, on FighterVerses.com, and as an app for smartphones and other mobile devices (IOS and Android in English, Spanish, French, and German). The Fighter Verses app includes review systems, quizzes, songs, a devotional, and other memory helps. For pre-readers, Foundation Verses uses simple images to help young children memorize 76 key verses. We also offer a study that corresponds to Set One of the Fighter Verses. Visit **FighterVerses.com** for more on the Fighter Verses Study, as well as a weekly devotional blog and free memory aids. See **Truth78.org/products** for more details on all Truth78 resources.

PARTNER WITH TRUTH78

There is a global need for solid biblical teaching that points the next generation to the glorious character and works of God so that they might "set their hope in God" and walk in His ways. Our commitment is to provide biblically sound resources for children and youth, as well as training materials that will not only serve North America but those around the world.

Will you help spread the testimony and the "glorious deeds" of God to the next generation so they may "set their hope in God"?

PRAY

Would you join us in making bold requests to the Lord?

- Pray that one generation will declare God's Word to the next and give us, as part of this generation, the grace to faithfully fulfill our responsibility and calling to the next.
- Pray that the Lord of the Harvest would send out workers into His harvest and equip us with all we need to do His will, keeping our hands to the plow until His work through us is done.
- Pray that the next generation will know and honor Jesus as their eternal treasure.
- Pray for increasing numbers of individuals, churches, and schools who are able to benefit from our resources.
- Pray for the continued efforts of translation teams and the establishment of new translation partners so that children around the world will have resources in their native language.
- Pray that the Lord would multiply praying and giving partners so that a rich harvest would be experienced by millions around the world.
- Pray for a growing network of individuals, churches, and Christian educators who are zealous for the discipleship of the next generation.

134

GIVE

Approximately 70% of our budget is funded through the sale of our resources. The other 30% is provided as God leads people to partner with us financially. This strategy allows us to fulfill our commitment to serve the Church while giving our partners who share this mission an opportunity to increase the impact of our ministry. Financial gifts allow for greater capacity to spread the vision broadly, produce affordable discipleship resources for the church and home, provide training to equip ministry leaders and parents, and distribute materials for our under-resourced brothers and sisters in North America and internationally.

We invite you to partner with us in this effort. Truth78 is a 501(c)(3) nonprofit ministry, making your gift tax deductible. You can find out more about giving at **Truth78.org/donate**.

*For more information on resources
and training materials contact:*

Truth78.org
info@Truth78.org
877.400.1414
@Truth78org